The Eleventh Plague

David Bowen

Little Skye Publishing

The Eleventh Plague

Little Skye Publishing

In this work of fiction, the characters, places and events are either the product of the author's imagination or they are used entirely fictitiously.

Cover Design by Reuben Whitehouse

‘*Praise for* David Bowen’

‘Intelligent prose combined with witty connotations. David Bowen’s style is wholly reminiscent of the post-Dickensian novelist Hanna Barbera’s very early works, particularly the mystery machine novelettes.’
The Angelic Times - Sunday Review Supplement.

‘Hell on Earth is one hell of a novel... Devilishly funny and fiendishly clever.’
The Mephistopheles Gazette.

‘In Angel Jenny, Bowen has created one of the sexiest babes to be found between the covers (of a book). Ten out of ten for phwoar factor.’
The Daily Saint.

‘The Eleventh Plague has some great puzzles that will keep even the most ardent cryptic clue connoisseur content.’
The Angelic Times’ Crossword Puzzlers’ Monthly Newsletter.

To Molly and Brian Griffiths
for their tireless research trying to
find the best ice-cream in Florence.

And Darrielle Cresswell
for the word plethora.

Acknowledgements:

Kath Cross and Ed Buchan for the fantastic support. Jon Morris because he has lots of money now. All the people who lent me their names so I could protect the innocent (you know who you are). Reuben Whitehouse at Rocketfuelled who took time out of his busy schedule to design the cover. The staff at the Waterloo Gardens Tea House and The Penylan Pantry who brought the coffee and were very quiet. And of course all those lovely readers who have been so supportive, in particular Shan Williams, Georgina Turpin and Ben Murray.

Author's Note:
The Eleventh Plague can be read as a stand alone novel. It is however, recommended that you read Hell on Earth first to fully enjoy the books in the order they were written.

The Eleventh Plague

Fact:

According to the scriptures there were only ten plagues of Ancient Egypt. Even in these enlightened times, academics and the Church alike still deny that an eleventh plague was created.

Galilei Galileo was a scientist, who came under close scrutiny of the Roman inquisition, leading to his house arrest in 1633.

The Swiss Army buy their knives from the two main producers of the Swiss Army Knife. They trade under the titles The Genuine and The Original. The army buys a strict fifty percent from both.

The cities of Geneva and Florence contain a number of buildings that could house terrorists. Both Geneva and Florence are still present to this very day.

Geneva is in Switzerland.

Architecture:

All descriptions of buildings, architecture and works of art contained within are fairly accurate at the time of writing. Although, I have been led to believe that the red door has since been painted blue.

Prologue

11.33 am, Thursday, 4th September 1400bc. (Give or take a couple of years).

Archangel Michael looked down the long table. He was relatively new to the job. Relative in the sense of immortality; where time takes on a slightly different slant to that of the mortal world. He had to admit he was not entirely comfortable with his new role. Administration and management did not really suit his personality. He was more your sort of *hands on* type of guy. He liked to get his hands dirty. He had certainly received plenty of criticism when he first became Head of Heaven. Many believed he was just too headstrong and rash for the job. When Satan had been naughty, he'd simply given him a good kicking and thrown him out of Heaven. Back then, there hadn't been any disciplinary forms to fill in or any strict procedures to follow, but times were changing. This was the future. He knew that. It was all about committee meetings.

The collected team of Angels and Archangels that sat either side of the long table, waited for Archangel Michael, Head of Heaven, to make his decision. The gathered ensemble represented some of the best minds in their fields. They were experts to the highest degree. Rarely were such specialists brought together. But this was important. It concerned what was commonly referred to as the Egyptian Problem. The Pharaoh had, despite numerous requests, refused to free Moses and his Israelite people from slavery and now it was time for direct action. Michael stretched his back slightly raising his shoulders.

'Okay, as far as a slogan goes, I think we should run with... *let my people go*. It's catchy and straight to the point. Well done.'

A dark haired Angel near the far end of the table received several words of congratulations and couple of hearty claps on his back from his nearby companions. Michael waited for the minor celebrations to subside.

'Right, now onto the persuasive incentive,' he snorted quietly to himself. It used to be called punishment, that is what it is plain and simple. 'In last weeks meeting we agreed to develop eleven plagues in increasing severity to *persuade* the Egyptians to comply. I gather we are on schedule?'

'All eleven have been developed and are ready for release as of tomorrow midday,' said an old grey haired Archangel raising slightly from his seated position, in order to pass a list along the table to Michael. He stroked his short neatly cropped beard thoughtfully for a second. 'Although, I do foresee a slight problem.'

'Yes?' said Michael looking up from the list.

'It's er, the eleventh plague on the list. I believe that perhaps it is a bit too severe? We are supposed to be the good guys after all.'

'Yes I see.'

'Yes, quite. We're a touch embarrassed about it actually. It was developed by a young biologist. My fault really; shouldn't have given the task to a novice, but we were pushed for time. Poor fellow had a bit of a breakdown. Bit of a shock when he realised what he'd actually created. Anyway, I was thinking that we should maybe put this one on the back burner. Save it for another day so to speak.'

'Of course. I think we have enough to be going on with. This one *death of the first born,* should be more than enough to persuade them to free the Israelites. Besides, the ten plagues of Egypt has a bit of a ring to it. Ten is more of a rounded number. In fact as a slight sideline I was thinking that we could go with ten commandments instead of the proposed nine.' Michael turned to an Angel on his right. 'Sarah, do you think you could rustle up another commandment? You're a parent, I'm sure you can think of something. Anyway, back to the agenda. In what order should we place these ten plagues?'

The old grey haired Archangel turned to his list.

'The plagues are as follows. Gnats, rivers of blood, death of cattle, death of first born, darkness; we thought a three day total blackout should suffice, boils, hail storm; we rustled up quite a good one for that, greatest storm Egypt will ever know, flies, as always the old favourite locusts, and er, frogs.'

'Frogs?' questioned Michael.

'Yes, we were running a bit thin on ideas.'

'Yes but a plague of frogs, not exactly a fearful punishment, I mean a persuasive incentive, is it? They just tend to jump around a lot.'

'Well lots of people are afraid of frogs,' blustered a red faced Angel on the right. 'Jumping around with their slimy skin. They give me the creeps.'

Michael turned his attention to the Angel.

'You developed the plague of frogs right?'

'Well yes as a matter of fact I did. But that doesn't make them any less frightening.'

'Okay we'll keep the frogs. We'll start with them. I think we should gradually increase the severity of the plagues anyway, ultimately ending in the death of all first born.'

'But you can't start with frogs. They're much worse

than flies, gnats and the odd bit of bad weather. With their hoppity hopping around the place,' the Angel said giving an involuntary shiver as he spoke. 'We should start with the gnats.'

'Hey!' said an olive skinned Angel further down the table. 'Gnats are much worse than frogs. And flies for that matter. Gnats give irritating little bites.'

'Nobody is frightened of gnats,' retorted the frog fearing Angel. 'Lots of people are scared of frogs.'

Michael banged his fist down on the table.

'Enough! I will choose the order. Anyway I've changed my mind. We will start with something a bit more dramatic. Give a bit of a punch to grab their attention early on. We'll start with rivers of blood.'

'Well if you want to start with something a bit punchy, perhaps frogs?'

Michael gave the frog hating Angel a look that spoke volumes. It spoke of a size ten shoe and a discomfort in sitting for a week or two.

'Right I believe we are done here. We'll start the plagues on Monday. Any questions?'

With no questions forthcoming Michael turned to the grey haired Archangel.

'Albert, can you please place this eleventh plague somewhere safe? The last thing we need is something like that getting unleashed upon the world.'

'Certainly. I have just the place. Completely secure. Beyond the wit of the most cunning thief or misfit so to speak.'

Chapter 1

3,414 years later (give or take a couple of years).

Bacchaus the Demon stood in front of the Fires of Damnation. It had been nearly eight months since the whole Hell on Earth fiasco. In that time he'd fallen from Head of Hell, to the lowly position of dragon dung slinger feeding the fires; to now, as the situation stood, a slave, slinging manure. The new Head of Hell had rightly deemed Bacchaus a threat to his position and as such had enslaved him. It just wouldn't do having such a dangerous Demon wandering freely around Hell.

Bacchaus put down his shovel and walked over to the rusty tap in the corner. Picking up his cup he filled it with the brown runny liquid which he hoped was water. If he bided his time, kept out of trouble, he'd reach parole in a couple of hundred years time. All he needed was patience. Trouble was as far as Bacchaus' virtues went, patience wasn't one of them. In fact if you were compiling a list of the Demon's virtues it would be a very small list indeed. It would comprise of none. Bacchaus just didn't do virtue. If you really had to pick a virtue, patience was the closest one he came to. Although it wasn't strictly patience, it was waiting. Bacchaus had waited for this opportunity.

Putting the cup down carefully, he pulled out a small handful of precious stones from his pocket. It had taken months sifting through the Dragon manure to find them. He crushed the quartz and amethyst to a fine dust and added it to the water. With the delicacy of a quality chef he sprinkled a small amount of sage into the mix.

The sage had been worth every penny of the bribe he'd given to obtain it. Just one ingredient left, and it was coming. Bacchaus went back to his shovelling.

The sound of the cast iron doors opening broke Bacchaus from his work. Two guards entered. The shorter of the two Demons carried a rusty tin tray with what passed for lunch in this place. His grotesquely twisted leg gave him a loping gait. Bacchaus watched as mucus dripped down onto the food from a large hole in the middle of his face which served as a nose. The other guard, the larger of the two, stood nearly a foot taller than Bacchaus, his large frame covered in short spiky horns. He would make a formidable opponent in a fight. Provided you fought fair. Bacchaus didn't fight fair. The two guards looked at each other grinning, obviously sharing a joke. The smaller one gave Bacchaus the tray.

'Remember you complained there wasn't enough salt last time? Well here you go,' said the shorter Demon with a nasal tone, which was quite an achievement considering his distinct lack of anything that could be considered as a nasal passage.

The short Demon pulled out a salt cellar. With a circling motion he poured the entire contents onto the meal, leaving a small mountain of salt on the plate.

'Is there enough salt for you now?' giggled the horned Demon.

Bacchaus took a small handful of salt from the plate and dropped it into his cup.

'Perfect thank you. Your name is Sarrgoth right?' he said looking at the large guard.

'Yes it is. And yours is slave.' Sarrgoth nudged his companion as if he'd cracked an hilarious joke.

The two Demon guards laughed and turned to leave.

'Oh Sarrgoth, do you know how I became Head of Hell?'

'No,' replied the Demon turning.
'Oh good.'
Sarrgoth turned to leave.
'Oh Sarrgoth, did you ever study occult chemistry?'
'No!'
'Didn't think so.'
Sarrgoth gave Bacchaus an angry glare and turned to leave again.
'Oh Sarrgoth.'
'What is it slave?' said Sarrgoth, his face ablaze with anger.
Bacchaus threw the contents of the cup into his face. The large Demon wiped his wet face and strode towards Bacchaus. He stopped his stride midpoint and looked down at his hand. The flesh slowly blistered and melted away exposing the off white bones beneath. With a low guttural scream Sarrgoth brought his hands to his face, his skin peeling apart revealing the skeletal bones beneath. The shorter Demon watched as Sarrgoth fell to his knees.
With a sudden blur of movement Bacchaus picked up the shovel and rammed the butt end into the stomach of the short Demon, sending him crumpling to the floor. Bacchaus twisted his grip on the shovel and brought it down onto the now prone Demon. With a relentless attack he brought the shovel down again and again. Blood sizzled as it splattered into the fire. Once satisfied, Bacchaus turned his attention to Sarrgoth. The skin and flesh had almost disappeared from his face and small pock marked holes were starting to appear over his skull. The horned Demon lay writhing in agony, a weak croaking gurgle rising from his throat. Bacchaus stood over his helpless victim.
'Let me tell you how I became Head of Hell. I put an occult potion in my predecessor's tea. A simple concoction but very effective. Works like acid. Had you

studied, you may have recognised it. Amethyst, quartz, sage, water, holy water is more effective but a bit difficult to get. And of course salt. Thanks for bringing that to me. Didn't you ever wonder why there's a superstition that a pinch of spilt salt should be thrown over your shoulder to keep the Devil away? Or for that matter why salt is often used to form a protective pentagram in Demon summoning? Salt is the binding ingredient. Had you studied you would have known that. You just can't underestimate the importance of a good education. Well as much as I would really enjoy watching your slow and very painful death, time is pressing.'

Bacchaus brought the shovel down. Stepping over the body of Sarrgoth he made his way to the open door, singing happily to himself as he went.

'Da da da da dum te dum te dum. Da da da da dum te dum te dum. I'm bbbbad, bbbbad, bbbbad. I'm bad to the bone. Bbbbad to the bone.'

Slyth, recently appointed new Head of Hell, sat at his desk. Slyth was not a particularly powerful Demon in the skull crushing sense of the word. His talents lay more in the form filling, law passing, sneaky creep direction. He was the sort that stuck a knife in the back of family, friends, and anyone else who was stupid enough to turn their exposed shoulder blades in his direction. Not that he was the sort to do it himself. That was far too risky for a snivelling git like him. Reaching for his pen, Slyth signed his latest law. He checked the carbon copy beneath before summoning his secretary via the intercom.

'Shatbutt, get in here!'

Although there was no reply, the polished dark-oak door to the office began to slowly open. Slyth looked up.

'Bacchaus!'

'Shatbutt has taken a sabbatical. Until his head grows back that is.'

'Guards! Guards!' Slyth turned towards Bacchaus. 'Guards?'

Bacchaus gave a slow sympathetic shake of his head. Not that he felt any sympathy. He just felt that the gesture added more malice to the situation. Slyth rose from his seat.

'Please don't get up,' said Bacchaus raising his palm and coming around to sit on the desk next to Slyth.

Slyth sat back down. He was, in essence, a glorified clerk. He was a pen pusher. He knew he didn't have the power to overcome Bacchaus. He had to buy some time.

'I was er, just thinking of you. I was thinking it was about time you were released and er, given your job back.'

Bacchaus casually picked up the pen from the desk and twiddled it between his fingers.

'Continue.'

'Well er, I've just been filling in. But I don't have your talents. I'm just a pen pusher, if you know what I mean. That's why they call me Slyth the pen pusher.'

Bacchaus smiled.

'Come now Slyth, we're all just pen pushers.'

As if to prove the point Bacchaus pushed the pen through Slyth's eye and into his brain. Shoving the body of Slyth to the floor, Bacchaus resumed his seat as Head of Hell.

Looking around his office he had two thoughts. Firstly, he'd have to punish those who had betrayed him during his downfall and secondly, his office would need to be refurbished. They were the same thought really.

Chapter 2

Death Number 221, formerly of the Human Transition Department, now Head of Plagues sat in his office. Perhaps the most important decision he had faced all week lay in front of him. It was crucial that he got this right. He had studied the numbers that lay on the document before him and had made his selection. He took the phone off hold.

'Okay. Give me numbers 9, 23, 25 and 42.'

'You want prawn cracker with that?'

'No thanks.'

'It'll be with you in twenty minute.'

'Okay, thank you.'

Twenty minutes. Death knew better than that. By some strange phenomenon every chinese takeaway known to mortal and immortal man was built in a temporal time warp. For some inconceivable reason time slowed down in takeaway establishments. Luckily Death knew this and made the quick calculation; twenty minutes in reality equated to thirty minutes in real time.

Death swung his feet onto his desk. That was the beauty of his job. There was never that much to do. The plagues' section was split into so many sub categories that Death's department only really dealt with the more traditional types of plagues; locusts, boils, rivers of blood, that sort of thing. Others had to deal with the more prevalent fields; such as biological weapons, influenza epidemics and animal diseases. As a Head of Department, Death 221 received all the benefits that such a job gave him. He got a decent wage, was invited to all the posh parties and generally received all the privileges that the job title provided. As the youngest ever Head of Department, he'd caused quite a stir in the outside realms. He'd even been listed number 97 in the Daily Saint's annual top 100 Bachelors of the Year pullout. Like everyone else who finds their name on those lists, Death told people it was just a silly thing. Privately, like everyone else in those lists, he was ecstatic that he was in one. Then later, like everyone else on those lists, he became concerned about the names that had been rated higher than him. Of course, he'd only got the job as a bribe to keep quiet about the whole Hell on Earth disaster, but Death didn't care.

However, it wasn't all the fringe benefits that made his job so great. The single thing, overriding everything else that made his job so great was his boss.

Death's boss was Pestilence (of Four Horsemen of the Apocalypse fame). In Death's mind the thing that made Pestilence such a great boss was the fact that he never actually turned up for work. Pestilence was a hypochondriac. If someone so much as sneezed in his vicinity, he became convinced that it was some highly contagious disease related to the umbola virus, that he now showed all the symptoms of having and would promptly take two weeks off work. This left Death 221 to run the department as he saw fit, which generally entailed playing games on his computer all day long. Today would be no different, or so he thought.

Milo was part-time temporary staff at the Plague Storage Facility. He didn't deserve this. He'd only taken the job to bring in some extra cash. He certainly shouldn't be responsible for something like this. The morning had been bad enough. Overnight some joker had opened one of the ancient plagues. Granted it hadn't been one of the messy ones, like frogs, but nevertheless it had been a hassle. Darkness. The whole facility had been plunged into darkness. It hadn't even been one of the more successful plagues of Ancient Egypt. Although, not widely known, the Plague of Darkness had been a complete failure. The trouble was that in Ancient Egypt there hadn't been any clocks. The only time recording device they had was based around the movement of the sun. Darkness blotted out the sun, and as a result, no-one actually knew the time. So when people woke up in the morning and it was still dark they just thought they'd woken up too early. Without any time keeping device to tell them differently they just went back to bed. The Ancient Egyptian Plague of Darkness, one of the ten great plagues, had merely meant that everyone had taken a three day lie in.

Milo didn't consider the futility of the Darkness Plague as he ran down the corridor. He had to find Death 221 Head of Plagues and quickly. This was bad, far too bad for a part-time temp to deal with.

Miss Lauren Holloway Death 221's personal secretary gave a light knock on her boss's door before entering without waiting for a reply. Death quickly slurped up the noodles dangling from his mouth. The sudden suck sent an arc of sauce skywards. Its journey ending neatly with a splatter on what may have been an important document lying previously undisturbed in the in-tray. Death briskly wiped his chin clean of the sauce too nervous to make the journey.

'Miss Holloway.'

'Sorry to disturb you, but Milo from the Plague Storage Facility is here to see you. He said it was very urgent.'

'Okay send him in.'

Death watched entranced as Miss Holloway left with a graceful turn, her long strawberry blonde hair following her movement a moment behind. He always said strawberry blonde when he referred to his secretary's hair. Ginger just didn't sound as politically correct somehow. Besides she was far too sexy to have ginger hair. He never minded being disturbed by Miss Holloway. His office always seemed a little brighter when she entered the room. She had a slender grace, yet at the same time a youthful aura that lifted the spirit. She also had very nice legs. It wasn't for that reason he'd employed her though. She could also type. With both fingers!

In contrast, Death didn't like being disturbed by Milo. It wasn't so much that Milo entered the room, as crashed in. Puffing and gasping in quick succession, his eyes rapidly scoured the room until they found Death. His general persona was similar to a cat that had recently experienced a detonated firework attached to its tail and is now fearing for the safety of its rectum.

'It's gone!'

Ah that explains it thought Death.

'What's gone?'

'It's gone, the plague is gone. It's just gone.'

'Okay calm down. Just explain, from the beginning, what has happened?'

Milo took two deep breaths before continuing.

'Well I came to work slightly early this morning, which was lucky because some idiot had released the Darkness Plague. Those jokers up on the fourth floor no doubt. So anyway I cleared that up with...'

'Okay. Let's forget the whole start at the beginning idea and say skip to about three quarters of the way through. You know the bit where the story has something that may actually be of interest.'

'Right, yes. Er. One of the Ancient Egyptian Plagues is missing.'

Death suddenly felt like a cat that knows November 5th (July 4th for American cats) is just around the corner.

'Which one?' Let it be frogs, please let it be frogs, or even flies.

'The Eleventh Plague.'

Death quickly did some arithmetic. Definitely ten. There were only ten plagues in Ancient Egypt, the idiot had miscounted.

'Milo. Milo,' said Death shaking his head. 'There were only ten plagues not eleven. So obviously you have miscounted.'

'No I mean the one they didn't use. You know the one that was too severe. The Eleventh Plague.'

'Oh yes of course, that one,' said Death calmly. 'Don't worry, I'm on it. If you could just wait outside my office a minute.'

'Sure.'

Death smiled serenely as Milo left the office. As the door closed Death sprang into action, muttering to himself.

'Shit. Shit. Eleventh Plague. What Eleventh Plague? Nobody told me about an Eleventh Plague.'

Death ripped open the bottom drawer of his desk throwing loose sheets and files out of the way until he found what he was looking for. He laid the file his predecessor had left him on the desk. In bold lettering across the front were the words "Things you really should know before you start this job." Death flipped it open to the index page.

Milo sat patiently outside Death's office. His eyes occasionally wandering to Miss Holloway's legs. He'd heard rumours that Death 221 had got the job in some shady back room deal, but now he knew the truth. The guy had instantly become his hero. The way he'd acted so calmly when he'd been told about the missing plague. If that plague fell into the wrong hands it would spell disaster. Disaster with a capital D, and misspelt with the letters o h s h i t in the middle. He was probably in there right now cooly taking control of the situation. That's how 221 had risen to Head of Plagues so quickly. Milo's thoughts were interrupted as Death raced passed him. His face reminded Milo of next door's cat that time when...

'What are you doing just sitting there? Come on!' shouted Death over his shoulder.

Chapter 3

Eleri Jones glanced at her watch as she entered the building. For once she wasn't late. Actually she was rarely late for any of her interviews. She was mostly running late. Running late was an entirely different thing to being late. It just meant that you had to move a bit faster to your next appointment. Eleri was used to moving a bit faster. It went with the territory. You're always in a rush when you're a journalist and Eleri Jones was a journalist. She was a journalist with the Angelic Times; the most prestigious newspaper in the afterlife. When people asked her what she did, she'd tell them "I'm a journalist for the Angelic Times." People were always suitably impressed. "Wow that's impressive, that must be really important" they'd reply. "Not really" she'd reply, and they, the people, would just think she was being modest. In her mind she wasn't being modest, she was simply telling the truth.

Eleri wrote the arrivals section of the Angelic Times. The worldly equivalent would be the obituaries. A short piece on what the new arrival had done in their life, what their hopes were for the future now that they were dead, and who they were not leaving behind but meeting. Okay so it wasn't a bad job, but she wanted so much more. She had ambition. She wanted to be a proper journalist. She wanted to find the story. She wanted to investigate things. Maybe this time she could sneak in a bit of real journalism, instead of the *fill in the blanks* standard pieces that she usually produced. Every time she tried it in the past she'd been quashed by her editor. Not that he was deliberately restricting her career, it was, as he always informed her, the arrivals section. This time might be different though; there was a discrepancy with the *new arrival's* documents. He was being held at the newly established Elvis Island until his papers were "all sorted out". There must be a story here somewhere thought Eleri as she entered the building.

The Elvis Island Facility had been created as a direct result of Reg Hallsworth's unfortunate relocation to Hell. It had been deemed that it might not be such a good idea to "let that sort of thing happen again." In the future any soul without the correct documentation should be held in a neutral facility until all the correct forms could be retrieved.

Elvis Island had been the perfect location. The building itself had been long established and could quickly be utilised. During the late 1970s and early 1980s, a number of sightings in local supermarkets of the late great Elvis had been reported. This caused some consternation over whether the King of popular music was in fact genuinely dead. Whilst an in-depth investigation took place, Elvis had been housed in a luxury building on the border of Heaven. Elvis Island, as it became known, was a huge mansion complex that afforded stunning views overlooking the Heavenly Realm. The large bay windows opened out to allow the sweet fresh air of Heaven to waft through the building and each dawn golden light filtered through the rooms. This was Elvis's house after all. Until its more recent role the building had remained unoccupied for many years, as it was quickly established that Elvis was in fact dead. Much to the relief of numerous heavenly souls who had purchased tickets for his forthcoming concert.

Eleri made her way to the reception desk, her heels providing a staccato accompaniment to her journey across the polished wooden floor. This certainly didn't feel like a *prison for Heaven seekers* as some of its more demonstrative critics had claimed. It felt more like a celebrity detox getaway; a prison you pay to stay at. The receptionist waited until the last possible second before looking up from her computer screen.

'May I help you?'

'Eleri Jones, Angelic Times.'

'Ah yes. We've been expecting you. Señor Phillipe Mangella is residing in the East wing. Straight up the stairs, second floor. Graham will show you the way. I'll buzz you in.'

The secretary leant down and pressed a button hidden under her desk. To her right a large set of ornate wooden doors gave a click in response.

'You can go through.'

On the other side of the doors Eleri was greeted by a young fresh faced Angel.

'Hello Miss Jones. I'm Graham. Here to see Señor Mangella I believe?'

It was a redundant question, seeing as she'd made an appointment and Señor Mangella was the first and only resident in the facility. Nevertheless, Eleri felt the need to answer it out of politeness if nothing else.

'Yes. That's right.'

Unfortunately, Graham belonged to that group of people who always feel the need to make small talk with strangers. As a trait this would not be so bad. However, these people rarely provide anything that could remotely pass as stimulating conversation. They rely on a collection of stock phrases which generally state the obvious, for example, nice/bad weather we're having this time of year, don't you think? Now this may seem innocuous enough, but it isn't. It is, in fact, a devious technique used to recruit members into their sect. Out of politeness you find yourself responding. Before you know it you yourself are making small talk with a stranger and you belong to them. Luckily, these people tend to be territorial and are therefore easy to evade. They rarely stray from their natural environment; such as bus stops and train stations, thereby providing a perfect reason why public transport should be avoided at all costs.

'Nice weather we're having for the time of year, don't you think?'

Graham's question was all the more pointless as Heaven and the surrounding area always had nice weather. Even the odd short shower of rain only existed to provide a multitude of rainbows a few seconds later.

'Er, yes.'

'So you work for the Angelic Times?'

'Er, yes.'

'Wow that's impressive.' commented Graham. 'That must be really important.'

'Not really.'

At times, (usually when confronted by a small-talker), it's amazing how quickly you can scale two flights of stairs and complete a short walk to the east wing of a building.

'Señor Mangella, the lady from the Times is here to see you,' said Graham leading Eleri down the east wing corridor. 'Señor Mangella?'

Graham's pace speeded up as he moved along the corridor, checking each room as he passed.

'Señor Mangella! Hello, Señor Mangella! He's gone! Mangella has left the building. Wait here.'

Eleri Jones listened to the sound of the young Angel running down the corridor back towards the reception. They say a good journalist has a nose for a story. She took a moment to breathe in the sweet almost intoxicating aroma of this story, then made her way back to one of the rooms they had passed. She was sure she'd noticed the curtain move slightly with a passing breeze. The window was open!

Leaning out of the window Eleri spied a drainpipe just to the right. One of the bolts fixing it to the wall appeared to be slightly pulled out. The bolt was weather tarnished and slightly rusty, apart from a small section about half an inch long. The shiny exposed section of thread still had stone dust clinging to it. Someone had climbed down it and recently. She removed her shoes and awkwardly scrambled out. Her left hand loosely holding her shoes, she reached across with her right hand and pulled herself onto the drainpipe. With a slight crunching scrape and a metallic echo that passed down the hollow pipe the bolt jerked out an inch further. With a muffled yelp, Eleri dropped her shoes and tightened her grip with both hands.

She watched her shoes descend the two stories and clatter onto the flagstones below. She wasn't really sure what rules governed death in the afterlife. She was pretty sure you couldn't die, but there again, she'd also heard a rumour that every time a shooting star is seen, it means an Angel has died. She was also sure that pain wasn't really restricted. She'd seen an Angel with a broken leg once. Looking down she felt that, at the very least, a lot of pain was on offer.

Eleri Jones had never attended Angel school. The only benefit she could see from being an Angel was having the addition of wings, and she'd never foreseen a situation where wings would be of any particular advantage. In her defence, few could claim that they would have foreseen the need for wings because one day they might be straddled to a drainpipe two stories up on a mansion on the border of Heaven. If they had they would most likely fit into one of these categories: A) They have a foresight beyond that of any reasonable perception. (In which case it may be beneficial to ask said person for next weeks lottery numbers). B) They belong to “Get Your Wings” Angel Recruitment Agency. C) They are lying. It is most probable that category C is also the reason behind the apparent perception in both categories A and B. Fortunately for Eleri there are times when a good grip, a rapid shimmy downwards, and a drainpipe can be an acceptable alternative to having a pair of wings.

Although the word unscathed can be used to describe most events in life, there are few times when it holds any significance. If you were to say you made it to the local shops and back for a pint of milk, the word unscathed would not be such a worthy declaration. If however, the route to the local shops happened to be in a war torn city and the road that contained the shop was referred to as *sniper's alley,* then unscathed is a relevant adjective.

Eleri made it to the bottom of the pipe unscathed. Picking up her shoes she made her way to a section of wall overgrown with ivy, also unscathed but far less relevantly. A set of footprints (that any crime detective novel would be proud of) in the flower bed underneath, confirmed her hunch. Señor Mangella had scaled the wall into Heaven. There was an unregistered soul walking freely in Heaven. She had her story. It was time to get back to the office and do a bit of background research on Mangella.

The office was surprisingly quiet. The usual rushing bustling reporters passing notes from desk to desk were absent. Eleri stopped a passing mail boy.

‘What's going on? Where is everybody?’

‘Haven't you heard. There's a big story breaking. Everybody's out trying to get the scoop. A plague has apparently gone missing. It's been stolen.’

‘Oh. Thanks,’ she said letting the mail boy go about his duties.

Eleri slumped down into the chair at her desk. A stolen plague. It was a big story. A huge story. Crime didn't often happen in the Heavenly Realm. It definitely overshadowed her story. Her dreams of a front page scoop began to evaporate. What were the odds on two *possibly* criminal events happening in Heaven? And on the same day! Actually what were the odds? Eleri sat up. Her computer sprang to life as she quickly did a search on Señor Phillipe Mangella. (It wasn't too happy about being woken up so rudely. It was having a nice dream about sexy mega bites, but hey that was life as a computer and right now it had a job to do). As she read Mangella's profile her blue eyes lit up. Eleri liked her eyes. As well as being really good at seeing things, they were also her favourite physical feature. They had a depth of colour similar to the ocean just before a storm arrives. Men often found themselves captivated by them, apart from sailors who for some reason just turned and ran screaming. On this occasion however, it was their ability to see things that she really liked.

Phillipe Mangella aka *the Jaguar* was a thief. He was a cat burglar. A prolific one at that; regarded as the bane of art collectors throughout Europe. He was also Catholic, and due to a significant display of repentance six months earlier had been granted a hearing for admission into Heaven. Strange thing was, Mangella was not dead. That's why his Confirmation of Death certificate had been missing. It didn't exist. Mangella had somehow faked his own death. A considerable achievement considering the strict guidelines laid down in the afterlife.

Chapter 4

Milo had trouble keeping up with Death. No matter how hard you try, you just can't out run death. Death pulled up sharply as he entered the rear entrance of the Plagues Storage Facility Building, causing Milo to collide with his back. In front of the two of them stood Pestilence.

'Oh. I thought you were off sick,' said Death slightly flustered.

'I was,' Pestilence gave an exaggerated cough. 'Listen to that. On my death bed. Then what happens?'

'You got better?' suggested Milo.

Death gave Milo a quick jab in the ribs.

'No I did not get better.'

'You are looking a bit under the weather. Maybe you should go back home?' The last thing Death wanted right now was his boss around.

'Well that's the problem isn't it. I can't. I've just had a phone call from Archangel Michael. Apparently one of the ancient plagues has gone missing. He's coming here now. And feel my forehead, it's all clammy. That's one of the definite symptoms of hypoglycaemia, acute hypoglycaemia. And I have to come here and deal with this. What I want to know is what the hell is going on?'

'Yes, indeed. That would be nice to know.' Archangel Michael had entered behind them. An old grey haired Archangel with a short cropped beard stood to his right.

'Er. One of the plagues is missing,' said Death.

'Yes I'm aware of that. And just for the record so is half the media who are currently camped outside the front of this building.'

'Outside this building?' queried Pestilence.

'Yes and I believe they are waiting for answers. Might I suggest a no comment at this stage?'

'Right yes.'

'Off you go then.' Michael dismissed Pestilence with a wave of his hand.

Pestilence brushed his hand through his hair and turned to Death and Milo.

'How do I look?'

'Ill,' they both replied in unison, as Pestilence left to confront the media.

'I'm sorry we haven't been introduced,' said Michael, his attention now on Milo.

'I'm Milo. I work in the plague facility, part-time,' added Milo hoping that his part-time status would relinquish him from any blame that might be hovering around.

'Ah Milo,' stated the Archangel standing next to Michael. 'I had a dog called Milo once, used to pee on the carpet. Milo's a good name for a dog though. Not that I'm calling you a dog, of course.'

'Yes quite,' interrupted Michael turning his attention back to Milo. 'Do you know what the Eleventh Plague actually is?'

'Er no.'

'Good. Let's keep it that way shall we?'

'Er yes.'

'Good lad. How about making us all a nice cup of tea?'

'Er yes of course.' Milo scurried off to make the tea. This was more like it. This is what part-time workers did. They made the tea when the boss arrived.

Michael waited for Milo to leave before turning to face Death.

'So. We appear to have a bit of a problem don't we?'

'Honestly it wasn't my fault.'

'No of course it wasn't your fault. It is however, your problem.'

'What?' Death's heart sank.

'You didn't read the small print on your employment contract did you?' Michael pulled out Death's contract from his inside pocket. 'It's here under stock control. You are in fact responsible for any missing items.'

'Oh.'

'Well why don't we start by trying to find out how the security was breached. Albert you were originally tasked with setting up the security on the plague.'

The grey haired Archangel stepped forward and gave a throat clearing cough before beginning.

'Indeed. Quite a challenge it was. A number of measures were taken to ensure the safety of the plague, so to speak. Beyond the wit of the most cunning thief I can tell you. Firstly, we marked the jar containing the plague with quite a bold sign saying *do not touch*. Not an ordinary jar mind you. It was one of those that you sort of have to press down and twist at the same time. Very clever and quite cunning I must say.' Albert gave a chuckle as he said this.

'A child safety lid you mean?' Death had a sinking feeling, he knew where this was going.

'Oh yes that's it. Name escaped me for a moment. But that's just the beginning. We also placed it on the highest shelf. Out of the reach of wandering hands, so to speak.'

Death waited a moment for Albert to continue with the list of security measures. They didn't come.

'Is that it?'

'Yes.' said Albert proudly.

'So in fact the security measures you set up...'

'Oh it wasn't just me, couldn't take all the credit.'

'...the security measures consisted of a label saying *do not touch*, a child proof lid and a top shelf. You haven't really had that much experience of those cunning thieves you mention have you?'

'Well not really. You don't think we've been out witted do you?'

'Several times I should imagine,' muttered Death.

'Oh dear, oh dear.'

Death watched as the veins in Archangel Michael's temple began to rise. Any second now there'd be an explosion. Michael had a reputation for his short temper. To his surprise Michael took a deep breath, visibly calmed and smiled at Albert.

'Not to worry, it's not your fault. We do after all rely on a certain amount of honesty here in Heaven. Now Death. I'm sure we can trust that you'll be able to retrieve the plague? Be a shame to lose your job over something like this.'

Death noted Michael's placid tone but knew better than to risk inspiring his wrath.

'No problemo.'

'Good. In your hands then. I'll leave Albert to fill in the details of the plague. I have an appointment to attend.'

As the Archangel left, Death noted his jaw clenching rapidly.

'So tell me all about this plague. What am I dealing with?'

'It's quite bad I'm afraid. It's depression.'

'That's not too bad. People have been dealing with depression for years. Death of the first born is much worse.'

'Not quite. We predict that thirty two percent of those affected will commit suicide within the first week. A further four percent will try and fail, which will probably depress them more.'

'What about using antidepressants? Can't we just put everybody on happy pills.'

'This I'm afraid, is depression in its purest form, so to speak. Remedies will be largely ineffectual.'

'What about some sort of quarantine?'

'Ah yes. That's another bit of a booby we made. Depression, as I'm sure you are aware, is commonly a symptom of circumstance or as a result of a chemical imbalance.'

Death couldn't help thinking that it was also spread through close contact with certain people. He knew lots of people that depressed the hell out of him.

'Not always.'

'No not always but mostly. But anyway er, here's the big problem. This depression is er, airborne. So it will kind of affect everyone. Bit silly of us really.'

'Okay this is a bit of a problem.'

'Quite depressing, so to speak. Excuse the pun.' Albert gave a little chuckle, but seeing Death's face decided to turn it into a little cough. 'No, no right. Yes, bit of a problem.'

'So do we have an antidote?'

'Ah yes glad you asked. Been working very hard on this one for a number of years. You see we realised that perhaps a joke would cheer people up a bit.'

'A joke?'

'Not just any old joke, a very funny joke. Funniest joke ever in fact. Quite ingenious wouldn't you say? Anyway our top minds have been working on it.'

'And do you have this joke?'

'Yes. Well not quite. Needs a bit of fine tuning. Lots of problems with all this political correctness and such.'

'Can I hear this joke?'

'Yes of course my dear boy.' Archangel Albert took a step back, stood up straight and puffed his chest out. 'Knock, knock.'

'Who's there?' Death waited for a reply. None came. 'Is that it?'

'Well so far yes. We experimented with what's the difference between, and how many something or others does it take to screw in a light bulb. But the unanimous decision was knock, knock was by far the funniest. What do you think?'

'I think I'd better retrieve this eleventh plague, quickly.'

'Oh. Yes quite, good plan. Shall we just carry on with the antidote in the mean time?'

Death couldn't decide whether he really wanted to answer that question.

Interestingly, Professor Cobblers found in a recent study on language that there is an imbalance between questions and answers. The problem lies in the fact that there are more questions than answers. This therefore explains why there will always be questions that remain unanswered throughout life. Basically there just are not enough answers to go around. Furthermore, Professor Cobblers put forward the theory that the use of rhetorical questions is in fact a subconscious attempt to readdress this balance, thereby leaving more answers available for answering the more important questions in life. Such as where did I leave my keys? Deliberately not answering questions was also highlighted as being an attempt at saving answers for a *rainy day*. Death didn't consider this when he finally decided to answer. It was more to do with his fear that this dotardly Archangel might stick around if he didn't get rid of him.

'Yes. That's a very good idea,' he said with an encouraging smile.

'Right, yes, good. One will leave you to it then, as they say. Good luck and all that.'

Milo arrived just in time to watch Archangel Albert leave. He looked down at the four cups of tea on the tray he was carrying.

'Oh has everyone gone? I made tea. What shall I do

with these now?'

Death quickly gulped down the four cups of tea in quick succession.

'Problem solved. Come on.'

As Death led the way to the interior storage facility from where the plague had gone missing, Milo marvelled at his problem solving abilities. With Death 221 in charge, they'd have this all wrapped up in no time.

'So any chance you can tell me what this eleventh plague actually is?' said Milo trying to keep up.

'No can do sorry. It's nearly top secret.'

'Nearly top secret?'

'Yep, that's even more secret than top secret.'

'Huh?'

'It's simple really. Top secret information commands a good price in the world of espionage *et cetera*. So people are always tempted to sell the secrets. Slightly less than top secret is not worth as much. So it's not really worth risking your career and reputation for and therefore much safer.'

'A reverse psychology sort of thing.'

'Yep. If people think it's not that important they're not that interested. If it has got for your eyes only on it, everybody wants to see it. If it says for your eyes only and maybe a couple of mates down the pub, nobody's interested.'

'Makes sense I suppose.'

'Not really. Anyway, how about telling me how you discovered that the plague was missing?'

'It was when I went to replace the darkness plague. I noticed the Eleventh Plague was missing from its usual place on the shelf.'

'Mmm. I think it's a bit of a coincidence that the Darkness Plague got released on the same day. Of course it's possible that the Eleventh Plague has been missing for some time. But I think that the darkness was used to cover up the missing plague.'

'It wasn't the guys on the fourth floor then?'

'No not this time. I think the same person or people are responsible. Ironically what they did to hide their crime actually brought attention to it. But you'd better go and check it wasn't just a prank. If you can do that, I'll make some enquiries back at my office. Give me a call if you find out anything.'

'Oh just one thing,' said Milo as he left for the fourth floor. 'The door was still locked when I came in this morning.'

The storage facility was vast. Grey metal shelves stood in uniform lines running down the length of the room. As Death made his way to the Ancient Plagues' section he tried to sort out his muddled thoughts. If the Darkness Plague hadn't been released they never would have noticed the missing plague. Death wasn't a big fan of irony. He'd seen too much in his time working in the Human Transition Department. Things just happened. Irony was just a word to try and make some sort of sense of what happened. The door was locked, which implied an inside job. But Death didn't think it was an inside job. He knew everyone who had access to this facility and trusted them all. The thief had somehow gained access. The first question was how? The answer presented itself almost immediately. Looking up to the top shelf where the plague had been kept Death noticed a skylight slightly ajar. Death climbed the ladder, that Milo had left, to the top shelf. The skylight was slightly to the right above the missing plague. A clear track had been left in the decades of dust that occupied the top shelf, confirming Death's belief that the thief had entered through the roof. He didn't take time to congratulate himself on his detective work, there were more important things to worry about. The trail of shiny exposed metal was roughly four feet across, passing numerous neatly stored plagues. The perpetrator had deliberately targeted the Eleventh Plague. Crawling on all fours Death followed the trail to the skylight, cursing as the knees of his suit became enveloped in dust. Jumping up he reached the frame of the skylight. Even with his height, he only just managed to grip the edge. Puffing with the unfamiliar exertion he pulled himself up and onto the roof. Whoever had committed the crime was some sort of acrobat. This was no amateur prank. This was a professional job. Looking around Death's heart sank. The trail ended right there on the roof. There was absolutely nothing to indicate anyone had ever been there. Even the gravel chips that covered the flat roof surface lay apparently undisturbed. It was definitely a professional crime. This was serious. Death had no idea whatsoever who could have committed it and, to make matters worse, his favourite suit had become dust soiled.

Archangel Michael had been five minutes late for his appointment. He hated tardiness and now he was guilty of it himself. Added to which the morning's events were causing a certain amount of consternation. A plague had gone missing! He tried to relax. He told himself to think positive thoughts. After all, he'd put Death 221 in charge. It didn't help. He sat up from his prone position on the couch.

'You seem slightly agitated. Anything you want to say?' The voice came from an Angel sitting opposite.

Michael looked across to the questioning Angel and laid back down on the couch. Therapy. Why did he, Archangel Michael, need therapy? Granted he did lose his temper on occasion, but that sort of came with the territory. He had a lot to deal with. No-one had suggested therapy when he'd lost his temper with Satan, but now they expected him to take an anger management course with Dr Reuben Von Hinkle.

'Tell me about your day,' suggested the therapist.

Death sat in his office. It had been almost an hour since Milo had phoned, confirming what Death already knew. Nobody was admitting to stealing the plague as a prank. If Death was honest with himself he didn't have a clue who had stolen it, but Death was rarely honest with himself. Quite simply an ego like his did not abide with honesty, especially concerning himself. Anyway something would turn up, it always did. So Death sat spinning in his chair constructively solving the problem by waiting for something to turn up. His lack of constructive thought was suddenly interrupted by Miss Holloway entering without knocking. Death immediately picked up a pen from the desk and began scribbling down notes and frowning in a seriously busy businesslike manner.

'There's a journalist here to see you.'

'Tell them no comment, and they can make up the rest.'

'She says it's important. She has information for you. Concerning the missing plague.'

'Okay send her in.' Yep. Something always turned up.

'You can see Death 221 now if you'd like to go through.'

Eleri Jones mouthed a thank you to Miss Holloway as she entered the office. She held out her hand to Death across the desk. He had a wide smile, the sort of smile that told her he was going to try and sell her something.

'Eleri Jones, Angelic Times.'

Death raised up from his seat and gave her hand a firm shake.

'Wow...'

Eleri knew what was coming next; that's impressive, that must be really important. It was always the same.

'...that's an unusual name,' continued Death. 'Eleri. I like it.'

'Oh. Er, thanks.'

'So you have some information for me?'

Eleri slid a folder across the desk towards Death. As he reached out for it she pulled it back.

'*Quid pro quo,*' said Eleri.

Death's latin was a touch rusty, so rusty he wasn't even sure it was latin but he had seen *Silence of the Lambs* so he kind of got the message. Eleri didn't speak latin so well either, but she'd also seen the film, and knew how this kind of thing should go. *Quid pro quo* was a posh way of saying I want something for this. Death and Eleri's eyes locked across the desk.

Death tried to evaluate the soul in front of him. She was cute, there was no denying that. Although she obviously tried to hide it. Her make-up was minimal and professional, and her hair appeared to be styled as somewhat of an afterthought. Death resisted the sudden urge to brush back a strand of her dark hair that had fallen softly across her face. This was a woman who wanted to be taken seriously, thought Death.

Eleri was also trying to evaluate the figure in front of her. Okay so he looked a bit like a door to door salesman, but in a strange way that added to his charm. She did have some prior knowledge about him. He'd been voted 97th in the Daily Saint's Bachelor of the Year pull-out. Not that she normally read those sort of articles, it was research, just keeping abreast of a rival's publication, she lied to herself. There was no denying it, Death was definitely a cool guy. Damn, she thought, she really should have made an effort, whilst trying to subtly flick a renegade strand of hair that had fallen across her face back into place.

Death broke the brief moment's silence.

'Okay, what do you want?'

'Information. I want to know what exactly this plague is. And I want exclusive rights on the story.'

'Well that will depend on what information you've got.'

Eleri slid the envelope back across the desk.

'Oh I think you'll be interested in this. It may just tell you who stole the plague.'

Death noted that she'd said stole. The official line was that it was just missing. She knew something. He eagerly opened the envelope.

'If it does, then we have a deal.'

Death took a few moments reading the printout of Mangella's file. Eleri took the opportunity to brush that annoying strand of hair back into place before Death looked up again.

'And this Mangella went missing last night?'

'Oh yes. Bit of a coincidence wouldn't you say?'

'Yep. I think Miss Jones you have yourself a deal.'

Eleri took out her note pad and pen.

'So where are you going to start your search?'

Death looked at the notepad in her hand.

'My exclusive starts here,' Eleri said responding to Death's unasked question.

'Well seeing as he faked his death. That would sort of imply that he is still alive. And correct me if I'm wrong, but most of the people still alive live on Earth. So I guess I'll start there.'

'Good. I'm coming with you.'

'You're what?'

'I'm coming with you. This is my story and I'm not letting it out of my sight.'

'What if I say no?'

'Then I'll just follow you around. Which is an inefficient way of doing things, and will probably be a hindrance to you, but I'll do it. Would it help if I said please?'

Death looked into Eleri's determined eyes. Her hair fell down across her face as she looked down; she had the sort of fringe that could never really make up its mind where it wanted to be.

'Please?' Eleri asked looking up through her hair in a fake girlish plea.

'Damn it.' Death knew it wasn't worth the hassle of arguing.

'Great. What's the plan?'

'Okay. Do you promise to do what I say, when I say it?'

'Of course. Well mostly.'

Death gave a sigh. 'Right well, I think I'll, we'll, need some help on this one. So I guess we had better start by reassembling the team.'

'The team?'

Chapter 5

Norris sat on the soft sandy beach, looking out to sea. Of course, the perceived softness of sand is largely based around its willingness to move out of the way, as it will freely yield under foot. It is by composition extremely hard; mostly made up from rocks and sharp bits of seashell. Few would champion the properties of a nice soft rock filled pillow, and yet somehow beaches get away with being described as soft and sandy. In this particular instance the beach is described as soft and sandy purely to perpetuate this perception.

The beach belonged to one of the many small islands that could be found in a region of the ocean near Fiji. Norris hadn't really found it, he'd sort of stumbled across it; his navigation skills were not in the same class as those people who found islands. His skills in that department more or less relied on pointing the boat in the direction of something big, like Australia, and continuing until you came across some sort of land mass. Like a small island with a soft sandy beach and much to his dismay, with nobody living on it.

Without dwelling too heavily on his present predicament, Norris had to admit the last eight months had been the best of his life. Well that's what he thought anyway. He couldn't really be sure about the first three or four years of his life. Maybe something fantastic had happened then, but he was pretty sure he would have remembered. He was definitely sane now, which was a good start. His insanity had jumped ship somewhere in the Pacific Ocean and was probably swimming around looking for someone else to be friends with. Oh yes, he was definitely sane. He did however, have a slightly different reality to all the other people who were sane. Perhaps the biggest difference between his and everybody else's, was the fact that his girlfriend was an Angel.

Angel Jenny had been the main reason why the last eight months had been the best of his life. Since he'd banished the Demonlord Bacchaus and saved mankind, although somewhat inadvertently but nevertheless very much welcomed, Angel Jenny had been his constant companion. The Heavenly Realm had considered the possibility that Norris may be subject to revenge from the Demon. They had therefore allowed Jenny to remain on Earth as his permanent Guardian Angel. They had both been overjoyed with the fortuitous decision. All the more fortuitous because Norris rarely benefited from anything that could be remotely considered good, average, or even slightly below average luck. His present predicament proved this.

Three days ago Jenny had gone home for the week to catch up with her friends. They'd agreed that Norris would continue sailing towards the next big land mass he came across and they'd meet back up there. Simple enough. Problem was that Norris' navigational skills were far superior to his actual sailing skills. He followed the basic principle that a boat was like a car. The hull was the wheels, the sails were like the engine that powered the car, and the steering wheel, well that was easy, that was the steering wheel. The first of his problems arrived when his boat had run out of petrol, namely the wind had died. Luckily, or what he'd considered luck at the time, the wind had died quite near a pleasant looking island, with a sandy beach. Using the yacht's engine, that did run on petrol not wind, he'd been able to hobble to the beach and park. Deciding to do a bit of exploring and camp the night, Norris took the limited provisions he needed and left the boat. The second of his problems arrived the following morning. The wind had picked up overnight, so he could continue on his journey. It was at this point that he noticed the second problem. His luxury yacht was nowhere to be seen. He'd forgotten to drop the anchor, or as he referred to it, put the hand brake on. Norris was marooned.

Norris was used to being alone; he'd spent most of his life alone, but now it was different. Jenny had changed that. He looked upon her in a glorious haze and every day away from her was like a thousand years wandering a dusty, arid land. Never before had he known the lightness of heart that each breath they shared could bring. And never before had he truly comprehended the meaning of the word lonely; until now. The worst thing was that there was no-one around to chat about his loneliness to. Well that wasn't strictly true; he did have Official Replica Fifa World Cup 2006 Football to talk to. Okay so it wasn't as catchy as Wilson, but he'd seen the film and got the basic principle of how the thing worked. Sadly, Official Replica Fifa World Cup 2006 Football didn't provide any constructive or meaningful responses; so Norris was left to ramble on alone about his loneliness.

'I never really knew what it was like to miss someone. It's like in every part of my body there's a part of her and now it's gone. Do you know what I mean?'

Official Replica Fifa World Cup 2006 Football didn't reply. Which Norris took as a good sign that his sanity was still hanging around. He picked up a handful of sand and let it run through his fingers. Brushing his hands free of the remaining sand in a determined manner, Norris stood up.

'You know what? I'm going to ask her to marry me. As soon as she comes back, I'm going to ask her.' Norris sat back down. 'Well no. I'll wait until the opportunity is right. That's probably better. Romantic sunset alone, something like that. But I am going to ask her. I don't know if Angels and mortals are even allowed to marry. But I can't see why not. You can be best man!'

Norris ignored the fleeting idea that Official Replica Fifa World Cup 2006 Football actually looked happy about the prospect of being best man. It was at this moment, much to his relief, surprise, and general panic, that the tip of a sail appeared on the horizon. The relief was provided by the thought that he might get rescued. The surprise was provided by the thought that he would be marooned for much longer than two days before a boat sailed past; in the film it had been more like three years. And the general panic was provided by the fact that he had no way of signalling the boat. As he gathered driftwood to make a signalling fire, Norris cursed his lax attitude. He should have got this ready. He should have been more productive. If it hadn't been for the scintillating conversation he probably would have. By the time he'd finished gathering enough driftwood for a small fire, the sail had become a lot bigger. So big it was no longer just any old sail. He recognised it as his sail. It was his boat. Norris lit the fire and began jumping up and down waving his arms. His first thought was that his boat had decided to come back for him. He quickly dismissed this in favour of the more probable thought that Jenny had found the boat and was coming back for him. As the boat came close enough to make out distinctive shapes this was replaced by a final thought; oh bugger! It wasn't that he didn't want to see him. Of course he did. Especially considering his present predicament. It was just that seeing him could only mean one thing; trouble.

'Ahoy there me matey! Avast. Brace the main sail, set the mizzen mast. Buy my crispy, golden, fishfingers and all that,' yelled Death as the yacht came alongside the beach.

'Does Jenny know you're here?'

'What's this? No hello Death so nice to see you? And no I thought she'd be with you.'

'She's visiting friends.'

'Well I'm sure she'll catch up with us.'

'Catch up with us? Where are we going? What are you doing here?'

Death ignored the questions. 'What still no nice to see you?'

'Why do people often say nice to see you?' Norris asked wading out to the yacht.

'Come to think of it, they don't,' said Death with a big grin.

Norris climbed the side ladder onto the yacht, and gave Death a big but decidedly manly hug.

'It's really good to see you! But I've got to ask, why are you here? Is something up?'

'Do I need a reason? I visited you guys a couple of months ago.'

'Yep. When you were hiding from that Angel you dumped. So can you honestly tell me you're not here because of some sort of trouble?'

'Absolutely. No trouble whatsoever. None. Zilch. Well maybe a little bit.'

'A little bit?'

'Okay so we've got big trouble.'

'We've?'

'Well I thought I'd bring the old team back together. Four musketeers and all that. Oh that reminds me, I've got someone for you to meet. Eleri!'

Eleri ascended from the lower cabin.

'This is Eleri Jones, a journalist for the Angelic Times. Eleri this is Norris, the famous mortal who saved the world.'

'Hi,' Norris was flattered by Death's description of him as saviour of the world; so much so, he forgot to comment on Eleri's job being exciting and that it must be really important. He also forgot to say no I'm not going with you this time, you wrecked my car and almost got me killed last time.

'Okay introductions made. Let's go and get Reg,' said Death as he pulled the yacht around and away from the bay.

'Just one thing. What are we doing?'

'An ancient plague has been stolen. We've got to get it back. If it gets released it'll mean the end of the world as we know it.'

'Oh, right. The usual then. Well at least you haven't dragged me into another one of your girlfriend crises.'

'We need to make a pan dimensional jump. Eleri drop the anchor when I steer us over the reef.'

'No wait. What reef?' said Norris a second too late, as a low grinding noise rose from the hull.

The yacht lurched to a wrenching stop as the anchor gripped tightly against the reef.

Chapter 6

Apart from the rocky start, the last eight months or so since his death had been the best of Reg's life. He'd got into Angel school and had loved every minute of it. And to top it all, he'd managed to get work experience as a Vengeance Angel. Okay so he'd had to embellish his C.V a bit, but who doesn't. He hadn't lied though; that sort of thing was frowned upon in Heaven. Being a Vengeance Angel was the most sought after job in the afterlife. What had swung it for Reg was his battle against the dark forces; namely kicking the Demon Bacchaus in the shin. Of course, he didn't mention that his role in the fight had mostly involved being thrown unceremoniously into Norris. But he was sure that that and his short essay on workers' rights had got him the placement.

This was his first proper assignment as a provisional Vengeance Angel. A group of teenagers had acquired an ancient summoning spell book and were about try it out. They had to be stopped just in case of the unlikely event that they succeeded in raising a Demon. Reg waited for his mentor, Gerald, to arrive.

Gerald had been described to Reg as the oldest, most respected Vengeance Angel in the business. The problem was that the adjective oldest over recent years had far supplanted the respected part of the statement. Gerald was similar to an ageing school teacher; whose years of dealing with troublesome pupils had left its mark. Gerald's nerves were in complete tatters; and a nervous disposition and being a Vengeance Angel didn't really go together. So it was that Gerald became a mentor to newly recruited Vengeance Angels. With the wealth of experience he was able to impart, he was an invaluable asset to the rookies' training. And it meant that he only had to deal with minor cases; like stopping a bunch of teenagers raising a Demon, which suited him just fine.

Gerald greeted Reg with a traditional handshake. The more modern Vengeance Angels tended to greet each other with *high fives* these days.

'Right then Reginald, are you ready to take on your first assignment?'

'Yes. Do you think we'll have to actually fight any Demons?'

Gerald's face blanched at the mention of a fight. 'No of course not. Well it's not likely, but I suppose they could have raised a Demon. Oh dear, you don't think so do you? Maybe we should get a move on. Stop them before they do. Grab hold of my sleeve and we'll make the jump.'

Reg duly held onto Gerald's sleeve. He hadn't passed his Pan Dimensional Jump Test and therefore without his licence was unable to make the jump on his own.

Like most forms of transportation pan dimensional jumping requires a certain amount of proficiency before it can be undertaken, and a full understanding of its theory is needed. *Pan Dimensional Jumping for Complete Beginners,* the highly regarded repository of knowledge on the subject describes it as thus:-

To fully understand the complex theory of pan dimensional jumping one must first adhere to the knowledge that everything is everywhere at the same time. In essence everything can be in more than one place at any one point in time. Equally so, it can also be nowhere, which sometimes makes it extremely difficult to find your car keys. (For further details of this, study quantum mechanics for twenty years). Naturally this gets quite complex when you consider that everywhere could in fact be in just one place. However, to the untrained eye it appears that everything is in different places rather than just one place. Once it is fully understood that everything and everywhere can be in just one place, it becomes easier to understand that time is the key factor that separates everything and everywhere into manageable segments. However, this may in fact be wrong, but don't worry about it, as it rarely comes up in the theory test, and you are better off spending your time productively; such as learning the stopping distances as this always comes up.

With the usual lack of anything remotely interesting happening during the jump, Reg and Gerald arrived at their destination. They stood outside an old wood panelled barn, its wood bleached silver by the sun. The sound of three voices chanting emanated from within. The chanting stopped abruptly, replaced with screams of terror and the sound of running feet.

'I think we may be a little late comrade.' Reg said moving cautiously towards the door.

'We might not be,' said Gerald hopefully. 'Have a peek, I'll wait here and cover the exit.'

As Reg moved to open the door Gerald moved back a pace or two. Yes definitely two paces back. The barn door burst open, throwing Reg backwards and causing Gerald to dive to the floor covering his head. Out ran three screaming teenagers (who cannot be named for legal reasons).

Reg poked his head through the now open door. As his eyes adjusted to the dim interior light he made out familiar shapes.

'What can you see?' asked Gerald from his relatively safe position.

'Hay bales, an old wooden ladder, various farming implements. Oh dear. And three pretty angry looking

Demons.'

Gerald was relieved. Three Demons was good. Had it only been one then his next statement would have made him look like a coward. But three, that was different. 'Okay, I suggest in my professional opinion that we run away and call for backup. Grab hold of my sleeve.'

As Reg reached out for Gerald's arm, one of the Demons smashed through the side of the barn, sending wooden shards exploding through the air. Reg let go of his grip to cover his head. When he raised it again Gerald was gone.

In fairness to Gerald, he didn't realise that Reg wasn't with him when he made the jump. Furthermore, in his haste he'd hadn't properly co-ordinated his jump and had no way of knowing where he had ended up. Therefore he had no way of getting back. Gerald made a phone call to his superior.

'It's Gerald here. I'm afraid it has happened again. I've lost another one.'

Reg was faced with three rather large Demons. All three looked the same with their grey skin and long tusk-like teeth hanging down over their lower lips. Reg didn't really think his kick them in the shins tactic would work this time, so he opted for a different approach.

'Demons of the Underworld, go back to where you came. Er, please.'

All credit to the Demons, they did consider Reg's request before they made their decision to stay.

'No.'

Reg couldn't help but feel that things didn't get much worse than this. As if to prove him wrong a fourth Demon turned up, slightly behind and to the right of him. He hadn't noticed the fourth Demon before; he looked different from the others, for one he was even bigger. His skin, that covered his huge veined muscles, was dark green and his nose was upturned revealing his very wide nostrils. His face was framed on either side with two twisted black horns. Even considering the other Demons, he still looked particularly mean. To Reg's surprise the fourth Demon strode straight past him and stood in front of the others, the huge frame of his back facing him. The other Demons looked slightly confused by this behaviour too. They looked even more confused when he grabbed two of them, slammed their heads together crushing their skulls and instantly banishing them. The third Demon's face barely had time to register its look of *even more confusion* before his neck was snapped and he joined the others. The fourth Demon turned to face Reg.

'Hello I'm Sam.' The Demon held out his hand in greeting.

'Back off Demon.'

'It's Sam.'

'Well then back off Sam. I'm not falling for any of your sneaky Demon tricks. I'll have you know I'm a Vengeance Angel.'

'Really?'

'Yes really. I'm a particularly tough Vengeance Angel at that!'

'Oh okay. It's just... oh doesn't matter.'

'Just what?'

'Well I was just watching you and that other one.'

'Yes and?'

'Well I thought Vengeance Angels could make pan dimensional jumps on their own.'

'Well I haven't passed my test yet,' Reg realised he may have said too much and quickly tried to make amends. 'But I'm so super tough they still need me.'

'Funny looked like you were about to run away.'

'Well that was to throw them off guard. So I could

strike. Look who are you?' Reg was getting a little bit confused and wasn't sure where the conversation was heading.

'I'm Sam.' The Demon held out his hand again.

For reasons that he would never be able to explain, Reg took the Demon's hand and shook it.

'I'm Reg.'

'Pleased to meet you Reg.'

'None of this is making sense. Why did you help me?'

'Just because we're Demons doesn't mean we're all bad. No wait, yes it does. I'm just, shall we say a bit different.'

'Why? You look very Demonlike.'

'Would it help if I changed into a human form?' Without waiting for a reply Sam transformed. In human form he looked the epitome of a gentle giant. He had a sort of dirty coloured blonde mop of hair and slightly rosy cheeks, capped off with a dim-witted toothy grin. 'Better?'

'Er, I think it would be better if you put some clothes on.'

'Oh yes.'

'I think I saw a pair of dungarees hanging up in the barn.'

'Right, won't be a minute.'

When Sam returned Reg couldn't help smiling. The dungarees only just reached past his knees; the image of a village yokel was complete.

'Sam? That's a bit of an unusual name for a Demon isn't it?'

'My real name is Guthra the Baby Slaughterer. I changed it when I had my epiphany.'

Reg was familiar with people having epiphanies. In his experience, largely revolving around Norris, it meant they went a little bit crazy.

'Your epiphany?'

'Yes. I came across this old battered book in Hell. It belonged to someone called Father Tobias, called the Bible. It was slightly burnt and had some pages missing but it changed my life. So I decided to turn over a new leaf. Like in the Bible, with Saul becoming Paul on the road to Damascus I changed my name when I saw the light. I wanted a biblical name, so now, I'm Sam the Baby Slaughterer.'

'Baby Slaughterer?'

'Oh yer. That's the family name. They never would have forgiven me if I dropped that bit. But Sam is short for Samaritan. Just like the Good Samaritan in the Bible. That's what I did when I saved you. I was being like the Good Samaritan...'

Yep I'm right thought Reg; epiphany meant as nutty as a Waldorf salad.

'...I'm trying to lead a good life, being kind to others, just like it says to do in the Bible. Then maybe one day I'll be able to go to Heaven. I don't think I'm very good at being a Christian yet though. I don't think I was really supposed to fight those Demons. I think I was supposed to turn the other cheek or something. But then I'm supposed to fight Satan's forces. It's all a bit confusing.'

'Yes it is, but I'm pretty sure you're allowed to hit Demons,' said Reg after a moments thought. 'Fighting the forces of evil is allowed.'

'What about humans? Am I allowed to hit them?'

'Not really, but it depends on the circumstances at the time. They have a place called Purgatory for all those little misdemeanours though.'

'Do they?'

'Yes.'

'Well that's handy. I think I might have committed a lot of those little misdemeanours.'

'I warn you, Purgatory is a boring place.'

'Oh. I could take a book I suppose. Is there a sequel to the Bible? I really enjoyed that one.'

There has in fact been great debate in recent years over a possible sequel to the Bible. Perhaps the most controversial being based around the rumour that God's apparent absence in world affairs is due to a large publishing firm's insistence that the world will just have to wait until they receive their manuscript; which is already over a millennium past its deadline.

Reg looked around at his surroundings. Apart from the barn, there appeared little to indicate where he was.

'You wouldn't happen to know where we are would you?'

'Yes. There's a small town nearby. I'll show you if you like?' replied Sam eagerly.

'That would be very, er, Christian of you comrade.'

'It's this way,' said the Demon with a beaming smile at being described as a Christian.

'Just a second,' said Reg remembering he had to retrieve the black magic book the teenagers had used.

Reg jogged into the barn and picked up the leather bound book that the teenagers had casually left discarded on the floor; an action mirroring that of any parent with offspring of a certain age. As he left the barn to rejoin Sam, Reg flicked through the pages of the book. He couldn't help thinking how irresponsible teenagers were. The book was a library book, and it was already two days past its due date! He faced a bit of a dilemma regarding the book. On the one hand, the book was extremely dangerous and could create an influx of Demons wandering freely around the world causing mayhem and destruction. On the other hand, it was a library book and you are supposed to return library books; it's how the whole thing works. Reg decided to keep hold of the book, even though in his mind this represented censorship, and in spite of his worry that they might insist he pay the late fees.

Sam waited for Reg to return from the barn near the dusty path that led to the town. It wasn't easy being a Demon and a Christian. They kind of went against each other. He kept on having to resist his more base urges, like running into the barn, ripping Reg's head off and using it as a football for an afternoon kick around; and he didn't even like football. Sam was strong willed though. He was determined to be a Christian, and Christians didn't play football with peoples' heads. Not the good Christians anyway. Good Christians gave money to charity, crossed the road to help others, and wrote letters to the Corinthians. Sam was determined to be a good Christian, although he was having trouble finding a postal address for the Corinthians.

'It's this way,' said Sam, as Reg reappeared from the barn. 'You're the first Angel I've ever met. Can we be friends?'

'I don't see why not. You did save my life, so that sort of makes us comrades,' replied Reg, as they began their walk to town. 'I'm not really an Angel yet though. I'm still in training, I haven't got my wings yet.'

'Doesn't matter. I haven't got any friends that live in Heaven either. So you can be my first friend in Heaven.'

Reg and Sam shook hands on their new-found friendship.

As they drew nearer the town the path slowly widened into a road. Eventually, it led them to a pleasant communal park that marked the boundary of the town. As the number of people increased Sam began to become nervous as he desperately tried to keep all his demonic urges under control. The ultimate test to his Christian beliefs came about as they passed a young mother pushing a small toddler in a pram. The child held a large lollypop in his hand. A temptation that pushed Sam's self-control to the limit. Don't steal the lollypop, don't steal the lollypop, he repeated in his head, whilst simultaneously digging his fingernails into his palm. Good Christians don't steal lollypops from toddlers.

'Is everything okay comrade?' Reg asked, as the mother and child passed by. 'You seem agitated.'

'I think I should be getting back,' said Sam, not wanting to admit his frailties to his new friend. 'They don't let us walk the Earth freely. We only get a short time. But if ever you need help fighting bad Demons give me a call. My secret Demon summoning name is Grupsparlardo. (N.B do not read this name out loud).

'I don't have a secret summoning name, but my mobile is 07700 900 555,' said Reg. 'Thanks again, for everything.'

With a sound like a rush of wind followed by the sharp snap of a whip Sam was gone.

Reg slumped down on a nearby bench that provided a view of the large manmade boating lake which had been strategically placed in the centre of the park for the enjoyment of visitors. He had no idea how to get back home. Maybe he'd be stuck wandering the Earth like Cain, doing good deeds wherever he went. As he thought about it Reg realised that wandering the Earth doing good deeds was a lot harder than it sounds. He couldn't help wondering what Death would do in this situation. Death would probably say to just sit around and wait for something to turn up. But that didn't really work in the real world.

Reg's thoughts were disrupted by a large luxury yacht appearing on the lake; much to the consternation of a young couple in a rowing boat. Whether their anxiety was due to its appearance out of thin air or the precipitous rocking it caused the small vessel in its wake, it was difficult to say. The luxury yacht cruised gracefully to the water's edge in front of Reg. A small crowd had gathered watching the strange events. The looming figure of Death appeared leaning over the starboard rail; with a quick motion he slung a rope ladder over the side.

'All aboard, who's coming aboard. Last stop before adventure and most probably misadventure.'

Reg jumped up and made his way to the boat. A man who had previously been happily feeding the ducks also approached the boat.

'No not you,' said Death.

With a look of disappointment the man returned to feeding the ducks, who had since decided to move on.

'What are you doing here?' Reg asked.

'Come on.'

Reg climbed up the ladder. The boat turned and vanished. The people who had gathered looked on in astonishment and cursed their luck. No-one would believe what they had seen and they'd probably spend the rest of their lives trying to convince others that it had actually happened. They were after all from a small town, and as such, nobody would ever believe them. Unusual occurrences happening to individuals in small towns were always passed off as examples of insanity of the said small town individual. Just like poor old crazy Jethro who claimed he'd been offered a job once in a newly built Hell situated in Utah. As one they decided the best course of action was probably to ignore the fact that they'd actually seen anything at all and to go back to their small town business.

Reg stood burning on the deck, as the sun blazed down. The sea lapped against the side of the boat; now drifting along with a slow current just off the coast of Southern France. He was a little bit peeved. No-one had bothered warning him that they were about to make a Pan Dimensional Jump and he hadn't prepared himself for the boredom of it. To make matters worse, after a very brief introduction to Eleri and a promise he would explain what was happening shortly, Death had disappeared to make a phone call; leaving Reg to suffer a guided tour of the boat by Norris.

'This side is called the starboard, no wait port side, no I was right first time starboard.'

Interestingly the term starboard comes from the Old English word *steor* meaning steering paddle and *bord* meaning side. Thus relating to the fact that boats were originally steered by a paddle held over the right-hand side. Thereby indicating the right side of a vessel. More recently the term has been used to alienate lily-livered landlubbers.

'So starboard is the left side. Why don't you just say that?'

'Well it's nautical isn't it. And look I managed to pick up a small submersible cheap on Ebay.' Norris proudly indicated what to Reg looked like a rusty old oil barrel with port holes and fins.

'Yeah it's nice. Have you used it to find any sunken treasure yet?'

'Well no. It needs a bit of a repair. It's perfectly sea worthy though,' Norris added quickly. 'The outside wheel thing for opening and closing is broken, so you can only lock it from the inside, but all the seals are intact.'

'That's not too bad.'

'Bit of a safety issue if something goes wrong though. You can't get to the person inside.'

'But you can go underwater with it?'

'Oh yes. Bit of a problem coming back up though. There's something wrong with the ballast tanks as well.'

'Oh right.'

'So that's my boat. What do you think? Obviously I don't normally have the bilge pumps on the go. We collided with a reef on our way to pick up you.'

Reg hated the display of bourgeoisie opulence; although he didn't begrudge Norris his reward for the trouble that they'd gone through. Privately he knew it was a touch of jealousy. His statue had turned out to be a bit of a disaster and he sort of wished he'd got the shiny red sports car instead. He quickly put his jealous thoughts to one side. Norris was his comrade.

'I think your yacht is fantastic.'

Chapter 7

Señor Phillipe Mangella lay still on the thinly padded plastic coated bed. He could sense his cold clinical surroundings without having to open his eyes. He was back on Earth. He hadn't wanted to come back. In Heaven he had felt true happiness that pervaded the very depths of his soul. For a moment, sitting on the roof of the Plagues Facility Building, he'd been tempted not to return, but he'd waited till they brought him back. He had to come back. His daughter needed him. His grip tightened around the cylinder he held in his hand. He'd kept his side of the bargain. It had been a surprisingly easy job. He was perhaps the world's most successful art thief after all; before he'd turned over a new leaf that was.

Phillipe *the Jaguar* Mangella had turned his back on his career twelve months previously. He knew he was a bad man; not the evil sadistic type of bad man. He never really hurt anyone, except financially that is; and then he hit them hard. But then most of the people who were victimised by the one man crime wave could afford it. It all changed when his daughter became sick.

It was at this point that Mangella had found religion. It had always been there, hiding in the shadows, ducking down behind a shrubbery when he turned. Ready to jump out and catch him unawares when the time was right; when his young daughter had been diagnosed with a brain tumour. For months Phillipe Mangella had sought out the best help that medical science could offer, to no avail. Then finally six months ago he'd turned to divine help, but his daughter still showed no sign of improving. Just as he had given up all hope *she* entered his life with a wide white-toothed grin, and hope returned. She'd promised that she could cure his daughter. All she wanted in return was a favour. Just one more job. She would be his daughter's saviour. She was Dr Laura Jane Welsh. Mangella opened his eyes.

Dr Laura Jane Welsh watched as Mangella slowly opened his eyes. Dr Welsh gave you an impression, you wouldn't immediately associate with a highly successful and intelligent scientist. She was more the type of person you thought of when you pictured a carefree young women making daisy chains in an open field. Her smiling face radiated innocence and her voice had a light inflection, rising at quite often inappropriate moments. She had the type of personality that you think you're marrying. If you had one word to sum up Dr Laura Jane Welsh it was lovely. If you had two words you'd probably go with really lovely.

There was however a problem with lovely Dr Welsh and that was what she referred to as Martha. You could describe Martha as the other side of Dr Welsh's personality. You would be wrong! Martha had no association with the personality of Laura, other than being its guiding force. Laura didn't do anything without Martha's permission. Martha's personality was dark and sinister. It was so dark it made black look like an off white colour that nobody really likes but improves the saleability of your house. It was Martha that was telling Dr Welsh what to do right now.

'Welcome back Phillipe.' She leaned into the metallic capsule in which Mangella was lying and carefully removed the container he was holding, placing it on a nearby steel table. 'Now I just have to give you a little injection to help with the transition.'

Mangella duly held out his arm. A slow numbness

spread through his body.

'I have done what you asked. Now will you save my daughter?'

'Ah yes about that. I'm afraid I told a little fib.'

Mangella tried to raise his body, it didn't respond. His brain panicked at his body's insubordination.

'What have you done?'

'Oh just a little something to incapacitate you. Nothing to worry about. We didn't want you to cause any problems. Couldn't have you wandering around freely, that just wouldn't do. Wouldn't do at all.'

'What about my daughter?' whispered Mangella, he was starting to lose consciousness he could feel the effect of the injection spreading.

'Oh I am sorry. There's nothing we can do for her. I'm afraid she will die a very slow and painful death.'

Dr Welsh watched, her head tilted to one side, as the muscles in Phillipe 'the Jaguar' Mangella's face relaxed and he fell into a comatose state. With the guiding hand of Martha she closed the capsule containing Mangella.

'Dr Hissel. Take over would you.'

Dr Wolfgang Hissel walked over to the side panel of the capsule. He smoothed down his already greased flat side parting. Although only just into his forties he had already made a name for himself in the scientific community. And now he had the honour and privilege of being invited into *The Trust,* under the mentorship of the brilliant Professor Maximillian Kloch. It was his groundbreaking work on cryonics that had made this whole thing possible. A low hiss emanated from the capsule as the seals did what seals do best and sealed.

Dr Welsh picked up the jar containing the Eleventh Plague and moved towards the door.

'Oh and be quick won't you. We have a train to catch.'

Chapter 8

Death hung up the phone and returned to the others.

'They have traced Mangella's soul. It turned up in Geneva for a brief moment before disappearing again.'

'How are we going to get there?' asked Norris.

Death looked up and down the deck then up at the sails. 'By boat.'

'Can we? I mean it's not like a car you can just park is it?'

'Don't worry they've got a lake.' Death paused at the blank look from Norris. 'It's called Lake Geneva, you may have heard of it.'

Norris felt slightly abashed by his distinct lack of geographical knowledge, especially considering his new career as a deep sea treasure hunter. He decided to try and make amends.

'Not a very imaginative name is it. Lake Geneva in Geneva.' He may have got away with it if he'd left it there, but he didn't. 'They must be really boring dull people the Austrians.'

'It's in Switzerland,' Death sighed.

'Yes and I'm sure the Swiss are boring too,' said Norris trying to dig himself out of a hole by digging at the sides to form a step like construction. A technique that is often overlooked by people who insist you can't dig yourself out of the proverbial hole.

'I don't know, they make those nifty knives that have loads of special tools attached.' Reg had always wanted a Swiss Army Knife as a boy, but had never got one. It still haunted him to this day. 'Maybe I could pick one up in Geneva.'

As well as being renowned as a good place to buy a knife with a little attachment for cutting your nails (and its beautiful lake), Geneva is also famous for having a convention. Any governing body that wants its sport to be taken seriously needs to establish a set of rules that the participants must adhere to. In 1864 it was decided that war needed such a set of rules, (particularly if it was going to be taken seriously from now on). So an international code was established in order to stop people cheating in war. It was called the Geneva Convention. After all, it was a convention and it was in Geneva, just like their lake (a bit dull perhaps but if something works just stick with it as the old Genevan saying goes). Strangely, more often than not it is the losing side that gets admonished for cheating, which raises the question of what is the point in cheating if you are going to lose anyway. The Swiss Army seem to care little about this anomaly, as they rarely get involved in wars these days. They much prefer to sit by their rather nice lake and play with their pretty nifty knives, which on the whole seems a much better way of doing things.

Reg was excited about getting his own pretty nifty knife but not so much that it stopped him asking a question that had been bothering him for some time now.

'Why do we need to make the jump in some sort of vehicle? Can't we just grab hold of your sleeve?'

'It's because of Norris. Mortals aren't able to make Pan Dimensional Jumps,' explained Death.

'But Norris has made the jump with us before.'

'That's because of the vehicle. It's the vehicle, be it a Volvo estate or a luxury yacht, that actually makes the jump. It just so happens that Norris is on board when the jump is made. So Norris isn't actually making a Pan Dimensional Jump, he only comes along for the ride.'

'That sounds like cheating to me.'

Before Reg could put in any further complaint, Death made the jump.

The clear blue waters of Lake Geneva parted as Norris' yacht appeared and then quickly resumed its state of tranquility. The same could not be said of the helmsman of a nearby sailing boat, who couldn't quite believe he hadn't noticed the 40ft vessel cruising towards him. Cursing as only an old sailor can, he swerved sharply to avoid its passage. The 40ft luxury yacht continued its gentle way towards a nearby jetty, amongst the distressed wails of 'woah, woah, woah,' the creaking complaints of scraping hulls, and Death's smiling greetings of 'ahoy there.'

Reg didn't even wait for Norris to put the *hand brake on* before jumping as gracefully as a short man with stubby legs can manage, onto the wooden planked jetty.

'Won't be long comrades. I'm just going to quickly pop into that shop while you tie her off.'

Norris gave Reg the *thumbs up*, on receiving what he could only imagine was a master mariners tip of tying the boat to the jetty. How did Reg know all this cool sailing stuff anyway?

Reg entered the fishing supplies shop that clearly displayed that they sold those pretty nifty knives that he was so desperate for.

'I'd like a Swiss army knife please.'

The ageing shop owner nodded knowingly as he bent down to the clear glass cabinet under the front desk.

'You're English correct?' he asked as he pulled out the display tray containing numerous little red knives.

Reg wasn't quite sure how he should respond to the question. He considered himself as English, but he now lived in Heaven. Did you remain English after you died? Or did you become a Heavenite? Was that the correct term? A Heavenite. A Heavenian, Heavenovian,

Heavenish. It was pretty confusing so he opted for 'Yes.'

'Which make were you wanting sir? The Genuine Swiss army knife or the Original Swiss army knife?'

'The one the Swiss army actually use.'

'They use both sir.'

The shop owner was in fact telling the truth. The Swiss army buy exactly fifty percent of their knives from each company. This is for the simple reason that they don't want to cause a fight. The Swiss army hate a fight.

Reg left the shop with his new knife and joined his comrades. Which make he bought will remain a secret to avoid any trouble.

As soon as Reg returned, Death led the waiting companions on the short walk away from the quayside to a leafy suburb near the centre of Geneva.

Cities have an inherent need to display their wealth, and they do this through their buildings. A city's buildings are like the tailor-made suits and the gold watches of the opulent. For older more venerable cities, like Geneva, large three storey town houses tell of a wealth of a previous age.

Death eventually stopped outside the entrance of a large imposing detached house. A low grey stone wall surrounded the grounds leading to two tall sandstone pillars, which held the intricate iron double gate. The building's flat fronted fascia gave it a somewhat functional appearance. It was reminiscent of the type of building that dealt with tax and duties for the Dutch East India Company in the mid-nineteenth century. Dark green shutters sealed the numerous windows, their paint dulled with age.

'This is it,' said Death.

As they walked up the grey stone chip driveway towards the building Pestilence opened the double doored entrance.

'What you doing here?' Death asked.

'I keep asking the same question. Every time I have to make a Pan Dimensional Jump I get this terrible headache. It's probably the sign of a brain tumour, I must get it checked out. Anyway, I'm sure you're too busy to hear about my suffering,' said Pestilence mournfully. 'Michael thought it might be a good idea to bring in an expert to help you, a Professor Theodore Bostock.'

Professor Theodore Bostock is considered to be one of the greatest minds ever to enter Heaven. He is also considered to be one of the most irritating. He regularly completes the Angelic Times' crossword in under ten minutes. Not that impressive you might think, lots of souls can do that. But he can do it with all the wrong words. Still not that impressive, that's even easier, you might be inclined to think. However, Professor Bostock completes the Angelic Times' crossword in under ten minutes, with all the wrong words, and still makes them fit the questions! He's so good at crosswords he doesn't even have to count out the number of letters in a word on his fingers.

'So what do we know?' asked Death.

Pestilence led them into the building as he explained.

'Well it's very strange. It appears that Mangella was the person who stole the plague. We managed to trace him to this building. It is registered under the name of Huey Rousso. The name unfortunately appears to be a fake one, probably Mangella used it himself.'

'So I take it Mangella has left here then,' remarked a disappointed Death.

'No he's still here.' Pestilence pointed to a large steel casket as they entered a large rectangular room to the right of the doorway. 'Unfortunately the plague isn't.'

The coffin shaped container had various dials and

brightly lit buttons covering its surface. Its left side was dominated by numerous pipes running into it from what appeared to be a large generator. Leaning over the casket stood an immortal soul wearing a black polar neck jumper, dark green corduroy trousers, and a tweed jacket. It was the sort of attire that someone who didn't believe clothes were important enough to disrupt their academic studies would wear; yet at the same time thought that a certain look was necessary to show that they believed this. Professor Theodore Bostock briefly looked up from his examination to give a mumbled greeting along the lines of 'grmm,' and ducked his head back down.

'Cryogenics! It's ingenious,' Death remarked.

'Why?' asked a confused Norris.

'Because if he was either alive or dead we could interview him to find out where the plague is. This way he's untouchable. Neither alive nor dead; just frozen in time.'

'Can't we just bring him out of it?'

'I'm afraid not.' Professor Bostock looked up. 'This technology is far beyond anything we can do. It is serious cutting edge stuff. Quite remarkable.' He turned to Death. 'Oh and it is cryonics not cryogenics.'

Death decided he didn't like Professor Bostock, it wasn't a difficult decision. He was the sort of person that liked to show that they were more intelligent than you. He'd come across plenty of his type in his previous job with Human Transition. They were generally the ones that would insist that they weren't dead and Death was obviously quite wrong.

'Nice corduroys!'

'Yes they're a narrow gauge tight weave.'

Typical thought Death. No matter how clever he was, he still wasn't smart enough to understand sarcasm. Death turned to the others.

'Okay. Let's do like Scooby Doo and look for clues. We need to find out where this plague is and if this Mangella was working alone. Pestilence do we know how he got into Heaven yet? Someone must have brought him.'

'Death 355 brought him in.'

'Typical. I hate that guy.'

'Doesn't that make 355 a bit, you know evil? He must have known something about it. Shouldn't he be punished?' Reg asked.

'See that's the problem with the Death department's position on neutrality,' Pestilence explained. 'Now take Death 221 here. He's far from neutral. He helped disrupt Bacchaus' plans for earthly domination. That puts him well and truly on the side of good, and there's plenty of others like him. So to keep the overall balance we need a couple of evil gits. By aiding a theft in Heaven, 355 has helped redress the balance.'

'I don't suppose 355 has come forward with any information?' Death looked hopefully at Pestilence.

'Nope. Like I said evil git.'

'I think it's bad news I'm afraid. There appears to be others involved,' commented Eleri, entering from an adjoining room.

'There is no way of knowing that,' retorted Professor Bostock.

'There are two used cups in the kitchen, through there. So it kind of points to more than one person.'

'Yes but maybe one person drank two cups of tea,' flustered Bostock.

'They only used one spoon. And from the smell I would say it was coffee.'

'Well that's not exactly a scientific approach. Maybe he used the same spoon two times,' snorted Bostock derisively.

'Yes that's true,' conceded Eleri. 'Of course, the one

did have lipstick stains on it. But scientifically Mangella could have put some lipstick on whilst drinking a cup of coffee.'

Death had to admit she was good. At that moment he felt like giving her a big kiss, which was funny because she wasn't his normal type. For one, she was obviously intelligent and generally he preferred the less obviously intelligent type. The type of girl that hid it so well you never got to realise she even had a brain that worked beyond the rudimentary functions needed to survive. But she had spotted a vital clue and made the Professor look stupid all in one go. He decided that he'd give her two thumbs up instead.

'Well it looks like we are dealing with a group. And although not a very scientific approach,' said Death looking at the professor as he spoke. 'I think we have to assume the worst. They are most likely a terrorist organisation.'

'I've found a clue! I've found a clue!' Norris said jumping up and down whilst waving a small piece of paper.

'What have you got there? Peace in our time?' Death said in his customary sarcastic tone.

'No it's a real clue. It's even addressed to us.'

'Addressed to us?'

'Well it says *for those who seek the plague* on the top.'

Death strode over and took the paper from Norris, and proceeded to read it out loud.

'For those who seek the plague. Give up your futile quest. The power belongs to us now. Best wishes the Galileist Trust.'

Professor Bostock came alongside Death.

'It can't be.'

'What can't be?'

'The Galileists.'

'Okay professor why not pretend that we don't

actually know who these Galileists are.'

'You've heard of Galilei Galileo though?'

'Yep. Scientist fella.'

'Well you probably know he was persecuted by the church for his views on the nature of the cosmos. The inquisition placed him under arrest. They set science back years. Then later, in the 1700's a group of scientists formed, called the Galileists, in recognition of Galileo. Their objective was to prove that God did not exist. Obviously the church took exception to this and condemned them, but in their attempt to destroy the organisation they merely drove it underground and into secrecy.'

'I was a member of an underground society in my youth,' said Reg. 'We used to meet in the basement cellar of the Three Feathers Inn. One of our members Nigel, his father used to be landlord at the pub. We were originally called The Society of Honest Working Masses Against Corrupt Capitalism, but we became The Movement of Honest Working Masses Against Corrupt Capitalism. We decided we were more of a secret underground movement than a society. Society just sounded too middle class.'

'Really, what happened?' Death asked, not through any real desire to hear more of Reg's story, but because of the irritated look on Bostock's face at the interruption to his own story.

'Well we had to disband in the end. Nigel's dad got caught for tax evasion, and he lost the pub. So we didn't have anywhere to meet. So the five of us went our separate ways.'

'There were only five of you! Not exactly working masses then.'

'Well we intended to get bigger. That's the trouble with being a secret society, it's really difficult to recruit new members if nobody knows you are there.'

Bostock gave a slight cough and continued, doing his best to ignore Reg and Death's interuptions. 'Trouble was, once the Galileists became a secret society, a bad element infiltrated their organisation and they turned to a more violent and aggressive approach. They became what we would now refer to as terrorists. Terrorists against the Church. Of course, the Church retaliated and an underground war ensued, until the Galileists were completely destroyed. For almost a hundred years there has been no mention of them, until now.'

'So what you're saying is,' Death paused. 'We are in the middle of some sort of conspiracy plot by an ancient secret organisation of scientists to destroy the Church.'

'Yes. I'm afraid it's looking like you were right,' said Bostock giving Eleri a nod. 'We're dealing with scientific terrorists.'

'That sounds a bit far fetched to me.'

Reg grabbed the paper from Death, quickly turning it over. 'Look there's something written on the back, really small, look.'

'What does it say?' asked Norris peering over Reg's shoulder.

'A plague in both your houses.'

'Oh. Doesn't tell us much.'

'On the contrary, I believe it tells us a lot.' Bostock adopted an aloof tone. 'I believe it tells us plenty. For starters the quote is from Shakespeare's Romeo and Juliet. Shakespeare and Galileo were born in the same year. Whoever left this is giving us a clue that the Galileists are involved.'

'I think they already told us that. Signing the note on the other side the Galileist Trust.' Death said.

'Yes but maybe the person involved didn't know the Galileists were going to own up to it. That's why the writing is so small. They didn't want anyone to notice they were leaving a clue! It would appear that we have an inside informer.'

'If this mystery person is on our side then why didn't they just tell us where they are?'

'That I do not know.'

'Really something you don't know? Eleri why don't you report that in your paper.'

'Actually I think the professor may have a point,' said Eleri reluctantly. She hated siding with Bostock. 'I think it is some sort of clue. The actual quote is a plague *on* both your houses or even *o* both your houses but never *in* both your houses.'

Eleri had studied Shakespeare; it hadn't helped her career or aided her in life whatsoever, until now. Ha! Who said that studying the classics would never be of use in real life. Now if only something to do with geometry would come up.

'Of course!' Bostock clicked his fingers. 'In, it says in.'

'Yes it says in. I get that. Maybe it's just a miss quote.' Death suggested.

'No it's deliberate. It's like a crossword puzzle.' Bostock noted the confused look from the others. 'In crossword puzzles the word *in* often acts as a preposition. It indicates that the answer is hidden somewhere within the following words. In this case it's probably an anagram. Unless it's our house, which I doubt.'

Norris laid down the paper on the steel casket and they all pondered the words.

'I can see the word route.' Reg said. 'And the word by. By route... Maybe it's telling us where they're going or what route they're taking.'

'What letters have we got left?' asked Norris.

'O, h, o, u, s and another s.'

'Oh.'

'It could be O.S as an abbreviation for ordinance survey.' suggested the Professor. 'That leaves us with h, o, u, s.'

'Sohu. By route O.S sohu!' Reg exclaimed.

'What's Sohu?' asked Death turning towards him for more information.

'Er. I don't know. I was hoping one of you would.'

'I think we've found ourselves at a dead end. Best to start again.'

The next several minutes were spent shouting out various individual words and the odd short incomplete sentences. None of which fitted. Professor Bostock was growing increasingly frustrated. The puzzle just didn't appear to have an answer that made sense. His reputation as winner of the Angelic Times' Crossword Puzzlers' Society's Annual Award for Outstanding Puzzling four years in a row was at stake here. Maybe he had got it wrong. Maybe it wasn't a clue. But, he never got things wrong. Then it came to him.

'Huey Rousso! Your houses. Huey Rousso.'

'The name used on the deeds to this house. You're right.' conceded Death.

'What about the letters in both? We haven't used them.' Reg complained.

'You don't have to use all the letters.' explained Bostock.

'You never said that. In that case it could be By route Hoss.'

'What's route Hoss?' asked Death turning to face Reg expectantly.

'Er, I don't know. I was hoping one of you would. Anyway if it is Huey Rousso it's not much of a clue. We already know Huey Rousso owns this house.'

The others disappointedly conceded that Reg had a point. Death picked the paper up and held it to the light.

'There must be more to it.'

Eleri's eyes suddenly lit up. 'Both! A plague in both your houses. Could there be two houses registered to Huey Rousso. They could be taking the plague to both the houses of Huey Rousso.'

'Easy to check,' Death said, patting Eleri on the shoulder. Death took a few steps away from the others, (more out of habit than any desire for privacy) pulled out his phone and hit the speed dial. 'Miss Holloway can you do a quick check for me.' He returned within minutes, his customary smile back in place. 'You were right! There's another house registered to Huey Rousso in Verona.'

Professor Bostock clicked his fingers. 'Verona. That's where Romeo and Juliet is set! I must admit that's a mighty fine clue.'

'Well I guess we'd better check out this house in Verona.' Death said clapping his hands together with enthusiasm.

'I don't suppose I could tag along with you fellows? I must admit that I find all this puzzle solving quite exhilarating.'

As much as Death found Bostock to be an irritating, pompous prat, he also knew he'd be handy to have around. He'd been in a *save the world* situation with Reg and Norris before and they had proved themselves; they had proved they were idiots. Granted they had come through successfully, but it had been one blunder after another that had won the day. Death was faced with the decision of increasing his chances of saving the world with an annoying prat or most likely failing but having more fun along the way.

'No. I think it's best you stay in Heaven. We're professionals at this sort of thing.'

Eleri jabbed Death in the ribs with her elbow. Which turned out to be a lot more pointy and boney than his first impression had led him to believe.

'What do you think you're playing at?' admonished Eleri in a whisper. 'You know if we're going to have any chance of retrieving the plague we're going to need him. And don't think I won't put in print that you were willing to risk the world just because you didn't want to hang out with a pompous ass. Because I will.'

'Actually come to think of it. I think you'd be a valuable asset to the team,' said Death turning to face Bostock.

'Of course I would. You quite obviously need my genius,' the Professor said, in what he believed to be a magnanimous gesture.

Death gave Eleri a look that said this is your fault. She replied with a look that said I'm sorry. Although it could have been a look that said I really think it's time we did the washing up; Death always had trouble differentiating between those two looks.

'What about you Pestilence? Are you joining us?'

'Oh dear, no. The air on Earth is so full of diseases I'm bound to contract something and hold up the mission. It's already playing havoc with my sinuses.'

'Okay then. If everyone's ready lets go save the world. Again.'

'What's going on?' said a voice from the doorway behind Death.

Norris dashed past Death and gave Angel Jenny a hug and a quick kiss. When they separated Jenny turned her attention to Death.

'Why are you here?' she demanded.

'Why are any of us here?' returned Death using what he perceived to be his profound voice.

'I'm not being existential. I'm being angry!'

One look at Jenny and Death knew she meant business as her bright blue eyes held his. Her usual smiling lips were pulled taut and her long flowing blonde hair was pulled up in a loose ponytail which bobbed with agitation as she spoke. The last time he'd seen her look like this she'd just been about to go into battle with the Demonlord Bacchaus.

'Er. Just a little adventure. Saving the world, that sort of thing. A plague has been stolen...'

'Yes I know all about the missing plague. What I want to know is why you've involved Norris? Don't you think I should have been informed? I am his Guardian Angel after all.'

'Oh come on Jenny it's not dangerous. You know the rules, we need a mortal guide. Interested parties should have a representative and all that.'

'Not dangerous! How do you know that? I've spent the last eight months keeping Norris out of danger. Making sure he stays hidden. Bacchaus wouldn't hesitate exacting his revenge if got the slightest chance. You know what he's like. Why couldn't you find someone else to join you on your little adventure? Correct me if I'm wrong but I believe that there's a few billion other mortals to choose from.'

'Bit under the thumb aren't we?' Reg whispered to Norris with a smirk.

'I heard that Reginald.' said Jenny

Reg slunk behind Norris. He'd heard stories about what happens when an Angel gets miffed.

'No he's right Jen. It's my life and my decision and I'm going to save the world.' Norris said his eyes locking with Jenny. Norris wasn't really sure why he'd suddenly decided to join the adventure. Up until this point he'd felt he'd somehow been tricked into joining Death.

'Well if that's how you feel I'm coming with you. Perhaps I can keep you lot out of trouble for once.'

'Woo hoo! The old team back together again,' Death said raising his hands in a silent cheer.

Jenny gave Death a cold stare but it only lasted a

moment as he held out his arms for a hug. Before she knew it her angry resolve crumbled and she was wrapped in his arms laughing. Despite her concerns about Norris' safety she was actually looking forward to hanging out with the boys again, and to saving mankind, it gave her a sense of purpose.

'So off to Verona then I guess,' said Death clapping his hands together.

'I've never been to Spain,' announced Norris.

'Italy,' corrected Jenny.

'No I've been to Italy.'

'Verona is in Italy.'

'Yes, I know that. I was just saying I've never been to Spain,' blustered a slightly red faced Norris.

'Just as a point of interest comrades. Seeing as we are going to Italy, does anyone speak Italian? Or maybe Spanish?' enquired Reg with a smirk on his face as he highlighted Norris' geographical failings.

'I speak Latin of course,' said Bostock.

'Problem is, we are heading to Verona and not the thirteenth century,' remarked Death. 'But don't worry I can converse in most languages. It sort of goes with the job. When I was with the Transition Department you never knew where you'd end up. I even speak tongues.'

'Tongues?' questioned Reg.

'Yer. You know. Like in the Bible. Speaking in tongues,' explained Death. 'Interesting language, caused a lot of problems in the ancient world though. When people started babbling in tongues it got a little bit confusing. See the problem is the language itself. Take *filba scabdon* that means pleased to meet you. Whereas *filba scabidon* means my wife is a trollop with a big fat nose. Basically when people started speaking in tongues pandemonium soon followed and a lot of divorces of course.'

'But you can speak Italian, right?'

'Yes of course. Well sort of.'

'Sort of?'

'I can say, bad luck you're dead, you'd better come with me. Oh and I can order coffee and kiwi fruit ice cream. If we get the chance, there's a great place that does an amazing ice cream in Florence. It's to die for. Sorry departmental joke.'

Chapter 9

Dr Welsh and Dr Hissel sat on opposite sides of the otherwise empty compartment. Their bodies giving a slow rocking motion in time with the train as it picked up speed. Dr Hissel was the first to speak.

'I must say it is an incredible honour being invited into the Galileist Trust. I've long been an admirer of Professor Maximillian Kloch's early work. It was such a shame that he moved out of the public sphere after er, the accident. May I ask, what is Professor Kloch like?'

'Oh yes of course, you haven't met him yet have you?'

'No. He wouldn't know me from Adam, he could pass me in the street and wouldn't have a clue who I was.'

'That's quite handy really.'

'Why?'

'Well I'm sure you realise it's an extremely secretive organisation. It's almost impossible to bring an outsider inside. And then you come along, an unknown scientist with a bit of knowledge that is crucial for the Galileist Trust's primary directive. Your work on cryonics was the missing piece to the jigsaw puzzle. They had no choice but to bring in a stranger based purely on my recommendation. None of the other members within the organisation know anything about you.'

'I never realised it was you who recommended me. Thank you.'

'Oh that's quite alright. It suited my purpose.'

'Your purpose?'

'Yes I needed to bring someone into the inner circles.'

'I don't understand, someone? Who me?'

Dr Wolfgang Hissel's confusion rapidly increased as the carriage door slid open.

'Ah Iscyrus. Your timing is impeccable, as always.'

'Who? What? I don't understan...'

As far as last words go Dr Wolfgang Hissel's were not the best.

Concerning trains. The modern train although highly efficient in taking one's self to a desired destination is not entirely conducive to the act of murder. Modern strip lighting negates the darkness that tunnels provide the would-be assailant. No longer can the screams of the victim be heard over the gentle rumble of the train's passage into darkness. Windows barely open wide enough to let a decent amount of air in, let alone throw a body out. No longer does a porter enter a carriage only to be embarrassingly fooled by the suspect kissing a random stranger; whose willing participation in the deception relies purely on the suspect's insistence that it's a matter of national security. Even Agatha Christie would find it difficult to instil a sense of *sinister romance* in a murder on a modern train. With this in mind, Dr Welsh and Iscyrus decided to instigate the cunning ruse of leaving Dr Hissel's body in the carriage as if he had merely fallen asleep, and hope that nobody noticed till they were long gone. Luckily for them, Poirot wasn't travelling on the train.

Dr Hissel looked down at his body. It looked as if he had fallen asleep. His out of body self told him different. He was dead. In spite of his recent demise he was quite pleased. This proved his current work in cryonics had been correct. Those cynics back at the institute had been wrong. There was life after death. A tall, narrow eyed man wearing a black suit entered the carriage. His upper lip sported a thin pencil moustache, which looked like it didn't really belong there. He reminded Hissel of a spiv from the 1940's. Hissel half expected the new arrival in the carriage to open his jacket to reveal a line of shiny gold watches hanging from the lining, or at least to offer him a pair of nylons using a whispered voice.

'Dr Hissel?'

'Er. Yes.'

'I'm Death number 355, Fourth Class, of the Human Transition Department. You're coming with me.'

'Yes, no wait. I've done something terrible, I need to warn someone.'

'Oh I'm well aware of what you've done. But we wouldn't want to spoil it by telling anyone else now would we? Besides if it is a confession you want to make there are plenty of people to confess to in Hell. Naturally they'd like to torture you for that information first though.'

Dr Hissel's screams fell on deaf ears as his soul was dragged to Hell.

Iscyrus listened to Hissel's last scream on mortal Earth as he exited the train with Dr Welsh and headed briskly towards the outside streets, and away from the station. They had followed the instructions to the letter.

'We work well as a team,' said Laura. But it was Martha that gave the voice words. The sweet side of Dr Welsh was deeply buried within her subconscious and it wasn't coming back now. Martha was in total control.

'Indeed we do,' agreed Iscyrus. His words belied his true feelings. How could a mortal even compare themselves to him. He chuckled inwardly. They never saw themselves as the expendable pawns that they actually were. This one's time would come, when she finally saw the truth, but not yet. She was still needed.

Bacchaus sat in his newly refurbished office. He had to admit there was definitely a positive side to having so many enemies. The positive side in this case was being able to use their skins to decorate the interior of his private quarters. He particularly liked the room's new flocked wallpaper.

'Bugflug, get in here,' Bacchaus commanded to the occupant of the adjoining room.

Bugflug the recently appointed personal assistant to the Demon Lord of the Underworld, lifted his large blubbery body out of the chair. He'd applied for the job through an advert in The Mephistopheles Gazette. He couldn't believe he'd got the job; with no previous experience and very limited typing skills he'd sailed through the rigorous interview process. The fact that Bugflug had been the only applicant had not occurred to him. Nobody ever went for this job; they only advertised as a legal requirement. Applicants for the job had previously been appointed on the basis that they'd been in the wrong place at the wrong time. Not deterred by the fate of his predecessors, he had been overjoyed to get the job. He was positive he wouldn't share their fate. The reason for this was simple. Bugflug was one of those rare and generally despised creatures in the Underworld. Bugflug was an optimist.

He was one of those who always viewed the glass as half full. This is often a misguided view of optimism. For a person to see a half full glass as something positive must surely rely on the contents of the said glass. If the glass is half full of some tasty carbonated beverage, then half full is definitely a positive outlook. If however, the said glass is half full of goat's urine, then half empty would be the optimistic outlook. Bugflug always viewed the glass as half full; after all, goat's urine might actually be quite tasty.

Bugflug entered the Demon Lord Bacchaus' private quarters confidently, the strides of his short stubby legs extended as wide as possible.

'Yes master?'

'Stand over by the window one minute would you.'

Bugflug duly responded to Bacchaus' request. Even with his overly endowed sense of optimism he knew better than to disobey any request from the Demon Lord.

'Now tell me,' continued Bacchaus pronouncing his words with clipped precision. 'Did you remember to send my instructions to Iscyrus?'

'Of course master.'

Damn his efficiency, thought Bacchaus. He'd only given that order five minutes ago. The nice new curtains he'd been hoping for would have to wait. Besides there were more important things to deal with than interior design. He knew he could rely on Iscyrus; he would tie up the loose ends, all of them, including Maximillian Kloch.

Maximillian Kloch was a genius. Not the sort of genius where you think wow, that guy is really clever. The sort of genius where you don't even realise that he's a genius because he's so clever you can't even comprehend that he is clever. Kloch's passion beyond everything else was science. If microbiology was a pie he'd have his finger in it, if nano technology was a pie he'd have his finger in it, if nuclear physics was a pie he'd have his finger in it. Basically, Kloch liked to keep all his fingers in all the science pies.

It was Kloch who reformed the Galileists. The accident had proved to be the driving force behind his decision to reform the long extinct organisation. It was the accident that had caused the death of his wife and unborn child. It was the accident that had left him in a wheelchair. It was the accident that caused him to turn his back on his belief in God.

The Galileist principles had been perfect for Kloch's

new perspective. He would bring the Church to its knees. He would prove that the God that had allowed his family to die, did not exist. Kloch spent every waking hour looking for evidence that God didn't exist. He also spent a considerable amount of his non-waking hours, as his studies invaded his dreams. Kloch became obsessed. He scoured every available resource in search of proof, encompassing Big Bang Theory, evolution, and even the strange phenomenon surrounding Tuesday afternoons. And then he found it; irrefutable evidence. Trouble was the result wasn't exactly what he had expected. Professor Maximillian Kloch born again atheist found proof that God did exist. Many would have expected the Church to be rather glad about this. It wasn't. The Church had built its foundations on faith, not proof. It even referred to itself as a Faith. Proof was the age old enemy of the Church. The Church relied on faith. And faith doesn't like proof one little bit, in fact they were arch-enemies. Professor Kloch's work kind of undermined everything the Church had been working on for all these years. The senior members of the clergy had no choice but to dismiss Kloch's work as another example of scientists interfering in God's business. The scientific world was equally dismissive; faith and proof did not mix.

Without any support and with enemies on either side, Kloch disappeared from the public world. He was alone. But now he had someone to blame for his misfortune. The evidence was there. God had done nothing to save his family and now Kloch would exact his revenge. He would undermine God's power. He would become more powerful than God. He would find a cure to God's greatest plague and make him impotent. And if he had any spare time left over, he would learn to play the harpsichord.

Chapter 10

The man strode across the bridge with the familiar air of someone who knows his surroundings better than anyone else. Certainly more so than the dozen or so people who followed closely behind him. His suit was Italian made and crisp. His shoes were Italian and polished, and he was Italian and fed up. In fact the only noticeable part of him that wasn't Italian was the bright fluorescent yellow bib; that was Korean or so the label informed him. He really hated that bib. It wasn't personal, the bib had done little to offend or cause affront. It was what the bib represented that he hated.

'And here ladies and gentlemen we stand upon the famous Ponte Scaligero; the Castelvecchio Bridge. It was originally constructed between 1354 and 1356 under Cangrande II della Scala. Sadly destroyed in 1945 during the war, it was lovingly reconstructed in 1951. This segmental arch bridge had the largest span of any bridge at the time of its original construction. An impressive 48.70 metres! The other two arches a still respectable 29.15 metres and...'

'Did Romeo and Juliet ever meet on this bridge?' the question came from a shabbily dressed woman in the middle of the less than enthralled group of tourists.

There it was, the reason why he hated the bib. It represented being an official tour guide for Verona Sightseeing Tours, established 1963. He loved the city with its fine art and stunning noble architecture. But nobody ever wanted to hear about that. All they were ever interested in was Romeo and Juliet. The highlight for them was standing under Juliet's balcony, so that their overweight, ageing husbands could *romantically* present a rose under a gaggle of tittering laughter, the whirring of cameras, and the inevitable comments of 'ooh doesn't your Fred look like a proper Romeo.' A proper Romeo with his scrawny legs, beer induced paunch and rumpled t-shirt. The majority hadn't even read, or seen Romeo and Juliet, they just bought into the romantic ideal. If they actually took time to think about the story they may actually see it for what it was. A couple of teenage tearaways sneaking out in the night behind their parents' backs, hanging out in gangs, getting into fights and stabbing each other. If that was now, Romeo would be busy trying to get Juliet drunk, and no doubt pregnant, in some local park.

'I believe Mercutio may have ridden his horse over this bridge.' responded the guide. His sarcasm lost in the unfamiliarity of his Italian accent. The bewildered blank stares from the assembled romantics confirmed his thoughts on their lack of Shakespearian education. 'Mercutio was Romeo's friend.'

Appreciative nods greeted him as the group looked around with new-found interest.

'The overall length of the bridge is 120 metres. Its two pylons reaching the impressive height of 17.2 metres and 19.51 metres,' continued the guide. His attention was suddenly drawn to a luxury yacht cruising towards them. Funny, he hadn't noticed it previously. With a sudden arm waving panic he leapt up and down yelling at the helmsman of the rapidly approaching boat. '*Diciannove metres! Diciannove metres!*.'

Norris turned towards Death who stood confidently at the big steering wheel thing.

'I think that man up on the bridge is shouting at us.'

'I believe you're right.'

'What's he saying?'

'It sounds like *Diciannove metres.* I believe it's some

sort of traditional greeting around here.'

'Oh.'

'Diciannove metres!' shouted Death waving his arms as enthusiastically as the man on the bridge. *'Diciannove metres!'*

'Er, Dickinovee meetres!' Norris joined the greeting. 'So what does it mean?'

'Nineteen metres.'

'Strange greeting.'

Professor Bostock casually wandered up to the helm, an unlit pipe dangling from his mouth. (He didn't smoke but felt the pipe added a certain gravitas to his outfit). 'Of course one could also presume that he is in fact warning you that the clearance on the bridge we are fast approaching is nineteen metres.'

Damn know-it-all thought Death.

'Well I suppose that's also a possibility too. But I'm pretty sure we can fit under that. And it is definitely a little known greeting of these parts. *Diciannove metres!'* responded Death with a smiling face and friendly wave before casually turning to Norris. 'Just out of curiosity what height is the mast on this vessel?'

'I'll check the manual.' Luckily Norris was the sort of experienced seafarer that found the need to always keep the manual close at hand. 'Seventeen metres.'

'See plenty of space,' said Death as the boat rapidly cruised towards the bridge.

'Would that be seventeen metres from the deck or sea level?' enquired Bostock.

Norris quickly flicked back to the relevant page. 'From the deck.'

'Ah. Then I believe, about turn, is the correct nautical term in this instance.'

Death's abrupt turn of the wheel was interrupted by an equally abrupt creaking cracking sound remarkably similar to the noise a mast would make colliding with a fourteenth century segmental arch bridge. The yacht came to a juddering halt halfway under the bridge, throwing everyone forward.

'Diciannove metres!' shouted Bostock to the people leaning over the bridge above them.

'My boat!' wailed Norris looking up at the cracked lopsided mast.

'Ah. Erm. Oops. Sorry. I'm sure we'll be able fix it. Sympathetic pat on the back. Oh wait.' Death patted Norris on the back. 'But right now I think it's best to make use of your dingy. We'll come back for your yacht later. It's just the Italians tend to get a bit touchy about people damaging their architecture. Come on everyone, abandon ship and all that.'

The companions quickly boarded the dingy, jostling to get into a suitable seating arrangement, before Death fired the engine. The motorised dingy sped them away from the scene, amidst the outraged yells of the gathered witnesses. As soon as they were a reasonable distance away Eleri pulled out her notepad.

'What are you writing?' asked Death suspiciously.

'Thought it might be a good time to write up the progress being made in our search for the plague.'

'Oh right. Well I do think we're getting somewhere. Don't you?'

'Oh yes definitely getting somewhere.'

'Good, good. I mean yes that was a little hiccup but we're on the right track. Aren't we?'

'Yes of course,' replied Eleri without looking up.

'It wouldn't really be necessary to include all the details really. Would it?'

'No not at all.'

'Oh okay. That's all right then.'

'Just one thing.'

'Yer?'

'How do you spell incompetent?'

Jenny couldn't help smirking as she looked across at Death's dismayed face.

'Looks like you've met your match,' she said sidling up next to Death at the rear of the dingy. 'She's nice though, don't you think?'

Jenny was in a successful relationship and as such she suddenly felt the urge to look at all her single friends as *possibly entering a relationship*, given the right amount of sagely advice from her of course.

Over recent years considerable scientific study has been given to this phenomenon. A group of like-minded scientists found that their respective partners suddenly displayed the desire to engage all their single friends in a match making process. They named the phenomenon Guilheim's Wife's Disorder (GWD); after a particularly nasty case of blind dates involving Kylie (from Professor Guilheim's wife's yoga class) and half the research team on the second floor.

Initial research showed that women appeared to be more susceptible to GWD, although the effect was not entirely exclusive to the female gender. It also became apparent that the affliction most commonly occured after approximately between six months to a year into a successful and happy relationship. Further studies showed that GWD was caused by a chemical imbalance in the mind that a happy relationship creates. Although why women are more susceptible to this imbalance has yet to be discovered. Numerous conclusions have been formed to explain the cause and effects of this chemical imbalance: That the sufferer apparently feels the almost overwhelming need to share the extreme happiness they are experiencing with the world. That by eliminating all the single women in the world they are ensuring their partners have no-one left to run off with. And the most popular premise; that they are getting bored with the relationship and need to find other couples to go out to dinner with. More recently the GWD has come into controversy however; when a group of like-minded single scientists dismissed the theory in a paper they published entitled 'Just Tell Your Bloody Wives To Stop Interfering With Our Lives.'

Death was definitely an advocate of the *interfering theory*.

'I think she's a journalist Jen. A heavenly journalist at that. Remember what they wrote about me. They said the only reason I got the job was because of some shady back room deal. You just can't trust journalists, they're always telling the truth.'

Death banked the motorised dingy sharply to the right, towards a section of the river bank with less of an incline. A trampled muddy slope between a copse of trees indicated that people used this section to access the river. A tangled rope dangled from one of the low hung branches to form a makeshift swing, its frayed end drifting in the water. Death scooped up the end of the rope and used it to tie the boat to the shoreline.

'Okay this is about as close as we're going to get to Huey Rousso's house.'

'So you know where we're going?' asked Norris as the group made their way up the slippery slope onto the streets of Verona. Although his own geographical skills were wanting, he knew enough to know that Death had got them lost numerous times in the past.

'Yes. Of course I do. During my time with the Human Transition Department I did a lot of work here. Romeo for one, he was one of my souls.'

'What Romeo and Juliet were real people?'

'Yep. Although not as the story would lead you to believe. In fact the two families got on tremendously well. As for Romeo, well he wasn't exactly your typical heartthrob shall we say.'

'What do you mean?'

'Well traditional heartthrobs, they're not exactly middle-aged men with beer induced paunches and scrawny legs. And scruffy, boy was he scruffy, the sort to wear a rumpled t-shirt wherever he went. Of course it was a rumpled doublet back then.'

'So what did Juliet see in him?' asked Norris.

'Well she was no oil painting herself...'

'Okay we get the picture,' interrupted Jenny. She liked the romantic ideal of Romeo and Juliet and didn't want it to turn out to be another Elizabeth Bennett and Mr Darcy. 'Is it much further to Huey Rousso's house?'

'Nope,' replied Death, leading them through a complex of straight lined streets away from the river bank.

Death stopped briefly at an intersection and looked at the house to his left, before taking a few rapid steps down the street to his right. The fading sunset gave the soft, salmon-pink houses of Verona an orange hue, as the companions made their way down the street behind him. Eventually, Death stopped outside a house with a bold red door. It was the type of red door that made you think blue would have been better.

'It's this one,' he announced triumphantly. 'Wait here.'

With a distinct lack of trumpet fanfares and flashes Death disappeared, leaving the rest standing outside the house. A few seconds later the front door to Huey Rousso's house opened.

'Come on everyone, inside,' said Death grinning. He couldn't help it, he loved mischief and adventure, and this was a mischievous adventure.

As the others passed Death into the hallway, Jenny reluctantly stepped forward.

'Should we be doing this? I mean it's breaking and entering.'

'No it's not,' replied Death still grinning. 'It's

entering. We haven't broken anything.'

'But this is someone's house. Somebody lives here,' said Jenny as she crossed the threshold.

'I'm pretty sure no-one lives here.' Death indicated to an adjacent room, its door wide open.

The others all followed Jenny's gaze into the room. The room was relatively ordinary for the type of residence it belonged to. It was slightly rectangular and furnished, albeit sparsely. It became instantly obvious that nobody lived there anymore. Dust had been left to settle. Cobwebs had begun to materialise in the corners of the ceiling and there was a subtle musty smell of emptiness. The resident had obviously departed in a hurry leaving his possessions in the house. They had not departed through any door though, red or otherwise. Inside sitting as comfortably as possible without the aid of gluteus maximus was a skeletal corpse.

'See I'm pretty sure no-one lives here. Well that guy doesn't anyway, I don't think he's lived anywhere in this world for quite some time.'

Norris leapt backwards at the sight of the skeleton, his foot knocking over a large vase holding numerous walking sticks. It gave a loud crash as it broke on the tiled hallway floor. Death gave him a withering look.

'Now it's entering and breaking. Granted, it's slightly different to breaking and entering, particularly in the order of things, but maybe we should try to be a bit quieter from now on.'

'Sorry I'm still not quite used to this whole dead people thing. You've had a lot more practise at it than me.'

'Okay let's start looking for clues,' suggested Death.

'I think I've already found one,' said Eleri pointing to the far wall. 'I just followed the skeleton's gaze.'

'Yes it's an oil painting,' said Bostock in his specially crafted condescending way. 'Of Galileo I would say, but I believe we have already established that we are dealing with the Galileists so not much of a surprise there.'

'Try looking a bit closer.'

'Well the brush stroke is quite refined. At a guess I would say early Dutch in origin. But not particularly remarkable.'

Eleri turned to the others. She gave a long drawn-out sigh at their dumbfounded expressions.

'This picture is square, but the marks on the wall show that previously there was a rectangular picture, see the outline where the paint's faded and the slight dust line. The picture has been replaced.'

'So they replaced the picture,' remarked Death.

'Yes and we're supposed to be looking for clues. And this grabbed my attention. Now look at the frame. It's got an inscription running around it!'

'You're really good at this,' said Jenny giving Eleri an encouraging smile.

Death walked up to the frame and read out the inscription to the others.

'For those who seek the plague: Behind the greatest of men secrets do hide. In part the root of all evil turns to entry. Ireanus' mistake does an answer provide. But the shape of these words are also the key. Inside pushy lock a clue to see.'

'It rhymes, that's clever,' commented Norris feeling he should at least give some positive input after the vase incident.

'Yes but the metre is all wrong,' observed Professor Bostock. 'English poetical metre is based on the Latin metre.'

In that short sentence the Professor highlighted two of Death's dislikes; Firstly why he disliked most poetry and secondly why he disliked the Professor.

'I don't think we need to critically appraise the

rhythmic qualities of the words, just solve them!'

'Well the greatest of men must surely be Jesus. But, seeing as we're dealing with the Galileists, the greatest of men is probably going to be Galileo himself,' said Jenny removing the picture from the wall.

Behind the painting embedded into the wall was the front of a safe, its edges lying flush to the wall itself. The only raised section had a key pad and a digital read out split into boxes, nine in total.

'I'm guessing the clue will give us the access code. Inside pushy lock, it's the keypad. Unless anyone here thinks differently?' Death briefly checked to see whether his companions were all in agreement. 'Well this Ireanus apparently provides an answer, anyone know who or what it is?'

'Maybe we could go ogle it using one of our phones or something?' suggested Norris.

'I think you mean google it,' snorted the Professor. 'It's pronounced google. It originated from a misspelling. They were referring to a googolplex, as in the very large number, it was something to do with their search engine program.'

'That doesn't make sense,' responded Norris. 'Go and ogle as in to look at something. Go ogle. Go look.'

'I'm with Norris on that one,' Death concurred. 'Ogle generally means to look at someone in a lewd way. And everyone knows the internet was invented by geeky scientists so they could perv on naked women all day.'

'No it is not! It's pronounced google and it derives from googolplex!' blustered Bostock. 'There is no gap between the go and ogle.'

'It's probably like the case of Bill Horley,' argued Death. 'Someone wrote Bill Horley the rapist on his wall but they didn't leave a big enough gap between the e and the r. People thought it said Bill Horley therapist, they started turning up at his house for therapy. He even had a couch bought especially, things were going well until that second conviction. Of course, if you want his advice now you'll have to go to the very depths of Hell.'

'That's like my old local GP. He listed himself as a notable doctor. Went out of business because everyone thought he was a not able doctor,' said Reg.

'Oh that's just like a restaurant near me. The sign said for a notable dining experience eat here. That went out of business too! Their sign-writer left too big a gap and it read for a no table dining experience. Nobody wants to eat out at a place with no tables,' added Eleri.

'See Bostock. It's more common than you think. But anyway this is wasting time. I'll just go ogle Ireanus on my phone.'

'Well the internet is no substitute for real knowledge,' grumbled Bostock.

'Do you know what or who Ireanus is?'

'No.'

'Right. Well in this case I would say it is a very good substitute.'

Professor Bostock wandered off in a sulk but not quite far enough not to hear the result of the internet search.

'Here we go. Saint Ireanus. He translated the Bible, most notably in Revelations thirteen. He altered the previous number of the beast from 616 to 666 because he felt the number had more of a ring to it and was surely meant to be that way.'

'So the number we need is 666. The root of all evil is the number of the beast!' exclaimed Jenny. 'That makes sense.'

'Problem is that's only three numbers and the code requires nine,' pointed out Eleri. 'There must be more numbers to get. Look, it says, but the shape of these words are also the key. Somewhere there must be more numbers in the actual words.'

As the others pondered over the problem, Bostock made his way back to them, in spite of his arrogant pride. After all, this was a puzzle and he liked nothing more than solving puzzles.

'May I see?'

Eleri passed the frame to the Professor.

'The frame is square' said Reg. 'So the words are shaped in a square and a square has four sides. Maybe the number four should be added.'

'Still not enough numbers though,' noted Death.

The answer suddenly came to Bostock with the word square. 'Ha! What we need here is some lateral thinking I believe. The words are in a square. The root of all evil is 666. So the square root of all evil. The square root of 666!'

Death began typing numbers into the calculator of his phone. 'I don't suppose you know the square root of 666?'

'Not off hand,' admitted Bostock.

'Well no problem my phone does. It's 25.8069758. Someone put them in. 2-5-8-0-6-9-7-5-8.'

Eleri pressed the key pad numbers. As she pressed the last number the safe door gave a satisfying click and opened slightly.

'Well done Professor,' said Death giving him a tap on the back. 'Excellent job.'

Professor Bostock hesitated for a moment. 'It was a team effort. I couldn't have solved it without Reg mentioning the square.' He had to admit to himself that humility did actually feel quite good. Maybe he'd try it again some time.

Eleri pulled the safe door open wide, allowing them to peer inside.

Their gathered faces registered disappointment as they viewed a single brown envelope in an otherwise empty safe. All except Reg of course, who was slightly too short to get a good view inside. Their general disappointment had little to do with their search for the plague, the envelope obviously contained a message. Their disappointment had more to do with the other element of the safe's interior... its emptiness. For some reason upon opening someone else's safe you expect to see treasures of untold worth; bundles of neatly stacked cash, uncut diamonds, or even the odd priceless family heirloom. Quite frankly, a little brown envelope doesn't live up to expectations.

'Oh well, better see what's inside,' muttered Death as he grabbed the envelope and opened it, revealing a single page letter. *'For those that seek the plague: Congratulations!'* Death resisted the urge to bin the letter immediately as is inherent when you open a mystery letter and one of the very first words you view is congratulations! Somehow he felt that this particular correspondence would not be offering a free luxury cruise. Instead he read on. *'We are impressed that you have got this far, but then we also expected you to. No doubt the Heavenly Realm has recruited its greatest minds to this cause.'* Death looked at the others, but for once managed not to comment. *'Apologies for being so cryptic up until this point but we had to ensure that the right people received this message. But now we're afraid, it is time to get serious. The Plague will be released on Wednesday at 5.30 p.m. unless our demands are met. You will provide our representative with the Secret of the Ages. You will give us the formula to life itself. An apt trade off we are sure you will agree with. The power of immortal life for a few or death for billions. The choice is yours. The trade will take place on Wednesday at 12 'o'clock midday on the terraced roof of the Bargello in Florence. Once our representative has the formula you will be given instructions to the location of the plague.'*

Death gave a groan and dipped his head as Jenny

vocalised his dismay.

'But there is no secret formula for life. People always think there's some mysterious answer. But there isn't. Life is just life.'

'I thought life was created?' questioned Norris.

'Yes life is created. Everything is created. It's just there is no formula for the creation of life.'

'That doesn't make sense.'

'Exactly,' groaned Death raising his head. 'It's not supposed to make sense. It'd be easy if it did. Any idiot could do it, we'd end up with complete chaos if life was being created all over the place. It's like death, there is no answer. Death is just death.'

'What about that monkey, Boo Boo. Didn't he write a book, *Life Explained* or something?' asked Reg.

'That was the purpose of life, not the reason for life,' explained Death.

'Hah! See I knew that a monkey wasn't the most intelligent being.'

Death let it pass. He had a more pressing problem. 'What we have here is a ransom that cannot be paid and the death of billions if we can't.'

Death gave a slight tremble as he spoke. The others saw it as an outward sign of distress at the thought of billions of innocent souls dying. Of course this was true, but Death's worry went deeper than that; just imagine the extra workload that would put on his department. Jenny put a gentle hand on his shoulder.

'I'm sure we can sort this out.'

'She's right,' encouraged Reg. 'Comrades all together. We stopped an apocalypse remember. I'm sure we can stop a group of scientists getting everyone down in the dumps.'

'Er actually might I make a suggestion?' As he spoke the Professor noticed that a bit of humility had found its way into his words again. A bit of humility was fine but he'd have to keep a close eye on things, it could get out of hand. Humility was no good for his academic standing whatsoever.

Death raised his eyebrows as a sign to continue. He still wasn't sure if he wanted to consider himself on speaking terms with the Professor, so decided to keep the words to a minimum.

'There may be a way of tracking the Galileists. We might be able to get to them before they can release the plague. A cohort of mine, Professor Guiseppe Caesaro is an expert on the Galileists. He spoke once of an ancient pathway to their headquarters.'

Reg figured the word cohort was the posh version of comrade.

'Go on,' Death figured this was worth being on speaking terms for.

'Well he said that a series of clues or markers lay where all could see, allowing prospective and like-minded individuals to follow the trail and find the Galileists. But it's better that he explains it, he lives nearby, and he is the expert not me.' Damn this humility.

'Okay lets visit this Professor Caesaro. It's a plan. It's not a great plan but it's still a plan. And from my experience not great plans seem to work out for us.'

'Slight problem. Guiseppe hasn't seen me since I died. It may come as a bit of a shock just turning up out of the blue.'

'Oh don't worry we're used to that sort of thing. People generally just take that sort of thing in their stride. Ask Norris here.'

'Er yer,' said Norris not really wanting to relive his experience. He knew now that he hadn't reacted very well when he'd been first visited by Reg. He decided to change the subject slightly. 'So how did you die? I mean if it's not too personal.'

'I was badly misinformed,' stated Bostock a slightly disgruntled look passing across his face. 'They told me I had a nut allergy.'

'I don't understand. How did that cause your death?'

'I consumed a packet of peanuts, collapsed, and the next minute I'm at the cattle grid to Heaven.'

'But they said you had a nut allergy.'

'Peanuts are not nuts, they're legumes! If I'd known I was allergic to legumes I wouldn't have gone near those pod encased bringers of death. You would have thought the medical profession would know the difference between a nut and a legume. Buffoons the lot of them.'

Death couldn't help but smirk. On the whole death was a serious business. It was usually quite tragic, causing pain and heartache. But every now and then you got a real hilarious one that made it all worth while.

'Well I guess we'd better get back to the boat and work out what we're going to do,' he said trying to hide his smile from the Professor who looked quite perturbed, which made it all the funnier.

Darkness had begun to fall as the companions made their way towards the dingy through the soft yellow lit streets of Verona. Cautiously in the growing darkness they made their way down the slippery slope and into the dingy. As they approached the yacht they became aware that it had attracted some unwanted attention from the local police. Standing on the bridge above the stricken vessel stood a lone member of Italy's finest. Although alone, they knew that one short word on his radio would bring his comrades out in force.

'Oh that's just great,' complained Norris. 'The police are guarding my boat. How are we going to get it back now?'

'Relax. If there's one thing I know it's how to distract an Italian,' said Death giving Jenny a mischievous grin. 'And you are that distraction.'

'I don't understand,' said Jenny, a puzzled look on her face.

'Let's just say he's Italian and you're a woman.'

'I could help,' suggested Eleri realising Death's plan.

'Possibly, but lets not risk it. Off you go Jen, we'll pick you up on the other side once we've got the yacht.'

Five minutes later, sitting quietly on the right bank, the group watched as Jenny made her way nervously across the bridge. She wasn't really sure how to be a seductress. She'd never tried distracting a man before. What Jenny didn't realise was that she distracted men all the time. She just did it naturally without noticing. Angel Jenny had a natural beauty and a grace that most women would die for; in fact most women would die, go to heaven and enlist in Angel School for. And only then realise that Jenny's grace and beauty didn't just come automatically with a pair of wings. Needless to say her slow stroll across the bridge caught the attention of the policeman guarding the yacht. All thoughts of his duty left him as Jenny glided past. He stood fixated at what could only be described as *an angel sent from Heaven* wandered casually past. A coy smile and a slight flick of her skirt was enough to break him from his google stance and sent him in pursuit. With the briefest of glances at the yacht below, the officer chased after Jenny.

'Ciao bella,' resonated through the night air. It was the signal the others had been waiting for.

It may appear to be stereotypical that an Italian policeman could be so easily distracted from his duty by a beautiful lady. However, the basis for a stereotype needs to be grounded in some truth or else it doesn't work. Luckily this policeman was that basis. Though in fairness there would be few in the male population who would not find themselves subject to this basis when Jenny walked past. It just so happens that Italians are more susceptible than most.

With the guard busily following Jenny down the street, the rest of the group boarded the yacht.

'So how are we going to make our escape? The mast is wedged tightly under this bridge?' Norris voiced his concerns to Death.

Death looked up at the slightly bent mast jammed fast under the arch of the bridge. 'Not a problem. Reg is already on it.'

'On what?'

'Well you know when a truck gets stuck under a low bridge. They just let some of the air out of the tyres and that lowers the vehicle enough to move it.'

'But we haven't got tyres. This is a boat.' Norris' nautical expertise was definitely improving.

'Yes but we're going to use the same principle.'

'How?'

'We're going to slightly sink your yacht.'

'How are we going to do that?'

As if in answer Reg appeared from below decks.

'I found these.' Reg held up a small axe and a fishing gaff in his hands.

Death took hold of the axe and followed Reg back down below deck. Norris following quickly in tow.

'Hey this is my yacht.'

'Relax. It'll only be a small hole. Easy to patch up,' said Death as he launched a vicious swing at the side of the boat.

'You said that about my car.'

'Yes and I got you this luxury yacht instead.'

'No you didn't.'

'Okay on a slight technicality, no I didn't. But you wouldn't have got it without me.' Death struck another hefty blow. 'Besides we all have to make sacrifices.'

'It appears that I'm the only one making the sacrifice here.'

'This suit,' Death pointed inwardly. 'This suit is not made for this kind of thing. Look the seams are already stretched. And it's not an off the peg number. This is a tailor made suit by Armando Vespucci from Magdalene Row.'

It should be noted that Magdalene Row is a short street in Heaven where the finest and most exclusive tailors can be found. There is approximately a seven month waiting list for a suit provided by one of its tailors. Which is considerably shorter than the waiting list for a hip operation. However, it is advisable to have the operation first as the suits are so bespoke the new hip may alter the exactness of the fit.

The street itself is aptly named after the Biblically famous Mary Magdalene, who many believed to be the finest *seamstress* of the time.

'Okay but do we really need to make another hole? It's still letting in water after the reef incident,' asked Norris as Reg rammed the gaff into the hole Death had made. 'Couldn't we just switch off the bilge pumps for a bit.'

'It'd take too long, we need a bigger hole.' Death struck another blow to emphasise his point.

'I must say I'm really impressed with your idea,' said Eleri as she joined them. 'And I intend to write up this whole episode in detail.'

Death stopped hacking at the side of the boat and casually leant against the side.

'Well you know, I pride myself on thinking a problem through quickly and efficiently.'

'Yes. Just one little thing I thought I might point out.'

'Of course.'

'You may have noticed that there isn't any actual water coming in through the hole.'

Death spun around and peered through the hole in the side of the boat.

'Just a suggestion, but you could try making the hole below water level,' said Eleri pulling out her notepad.

Reg gave a knowing nod which translated verbally would have gone something like; *you know what? I think you're right, good idea.* And proceeded to make a hole a bit lower down.

Bostock sitting nearby scribbling in a notepad gave a chuckle.

'Well you didn't realise either,' said Death.

'I did actually.'

'Why didn't you point it out earlier then?'

'I've been busy. You realise there is an alternative way of lowering the yacht. Without so many holes. All we had to do was increase the load, the extra weight would have made us lie deeper in the water.'

'Why didn't you point that out?'

'Well I needed to work out the exact logistics of it. Here,' the Professor pointed to his pad. 'It's the scientific formula for the weight mass ratio needed.'

Death looked at the pad. The Professor's scribbling looked scientific and correct, but he couldn't tell the difference. It could mean anything as far as he was concerned. Suddenly, the shining light of inventiveness entered Death's mind, and it brought with it a plan.

'You can write a scientific formula?'

'Yes, naturally.'

'Then you could write up a formula for the secret of life to give to the Galileists.'

'Well I think that is beyond even my talents. I believe we established there is no formula. Even if there was, to have it ready by wednesday twelve noon would be a bit of a push.'

'Don't you see. It doesn't have to be real. Just convincing enough at first glance. Something to buy us some time. But first we need to get moving. Reg how you getting on?'

'Nearly through...aghh,' cried Reg as a blast of water sprayed into his face from the breached hull.

Reg stepped back admiring his work, as water flooded in covering the lower deck's floor.

'It's working,' shouted Eleri from above. 'We're almost free. In fact, I think it might be working a bit too well.'

'Um the hole seems quite big actually,' said a soaking wet Reg from below.

'Oh.' Death turned to Norris. 'I think you should perhaps plug up the hole now. You know, before we fully sink.'

'With what?'

'Oh I'm sure there'll be some sort of kit stored below. Even bicycles have puncture repair kits and this is a luxury yacht.'

Norris raced down the steps. The sound of frantic cupboard opening and crashing followed. Death quickly made his way to the dingy before the gushing water soaked his suit.

'Okay then. I'll get Jenny, while the rest of you get us free from this bridge. We'll meet up stream,' Death paused. 'Oh and someone tell Norris upstream is that way.'

Jenny had walked some distance up the left bank, the policeman always behind. Despite the numerous twists and turns of the city's streets he always seemed to find her. The officer of the law had spent years honing his skills of pursuit. If he put half the effort into catching criminals there would be a zero crime rate in the city.

'Ahoy there!' shouted Death to gain her attention (in the age old manner of seafarers amongst whom he now considered himself).

Jenny rushed down to the dingy and lightly skipped onboard.

'Quickly, he's still close behind. Got to give it to him for being persistent.'

'Well he would be, he's Italian. Did you know there's two hundred and fifty two ways to ask for sex in Italian but only two hundred and thirty five ways to say no? That's why they're so persistent. They keep trying on the off chance they'll come across one of the ways that you can't reply no to.'

'Seriously?'

'I'm always serious,' said Death smirking. 'I'm Death and you don't get more serious than that!'

Death fired the engine of the dingy and headed towards the yacht which was now slowly making its way along the river.

The Italian policeman was less than fifty metres away when he realised his crucial mistake. Sprinting to the riverbank, he watched helplessly as Jenny and Death climbed aboard the yacht and disappeared into the blackness. Disconsolately he unhooked his radio. He'd have to tell his superior.

'Sergeant Carponi. I have made the most terrible mistake! I have seen the most beautiful woman, but I have lost her. She was an angel. An angel who would make other angels weep at her beauty. I will never again see her like in this world or the next.'

Sergeant Carponi would understand; after all, he was Italian too.

Chapter 11

Father Francesco Baggio drove along the dusty country road just outside the small Italian town where he lived. The old Fiat had served him well over the years, but now it struggled as it faced the steep incline of the mountainside.

'Come on old friend not much further now,' said Father Baggio tapping the steering wheel.

Slight beads of sweat had begun to appear on the priest's forehead. It was a hot day and the car only had the most basic of air conditioning systems; winding the window down made it cooler and winding it up made it warmer. Father Baggio tilted his head out of the window and felt the cooling breeze. It was a beautiful sunny day in the most idyllic of settings. Father Baggio gave thanks to the Lord for giving him this parish in Tuscany.

Father Francesco Baggio was a soldier of God. Not the sort of soldier who would ever be recognised for his deeds. He would never be acclaimed for his exceptional works, rise to the higher orders of the church, or become canonised. There would never be impressive statues commemorating Saint Baggio of Tuscany. Father Baggio was a simple foot soldier of God. He was merely a single digit in the record books. Similar to the single digits found in history books about some war; 6,516 troops died during this battle. Baggio was not a general or an exponent of great deeds. No chapter would be devoted to him. He was what could be termed cannon fodder, just another digit making up a number of casualties in the battle between good and evil. But he liked it that way, he had no desire for advancement. He just enjoyed serving the people of his parish, the people he loved, in the name of God. Father Francesco Baggio was a good man.

Baggio had joined the priesthood as a young man over twenty years ago. Perhaps the greatest influence on Francesco's choice to spend his life serving God had been his grandmother. Nana Baggio had always been a devoted Christian and her faith had rubbed off on the young Francesco. Nana Baggio had always insisted that he had her gift to see evil wherever it lurked. She had eventually gone to a *special quiet place for people with her gift,* after she saw the evil mark on a visiting bishop. She passed away two years later, long before the bishop had been found with those photographs. The young Francesco had wanted to tell people that he had the gift too. He wanted to go to the *special quiet place,* where there was always lots to do. You could paint and draw, there was always lots of crayons, and there was a big garden to walk around. They even brought your dinner on a clean and shiny white plastic plate with compartments for all the different food. But Nana Baggio had made him promise he'd never tell he had the gift, and he never did.

With a valiant effort the car eventually reached the crossroads. Baggio was faced with a choice. He wanted to visit two of the parishioners today. To the right was a young family that had fallen on hard times. Over the years he had saved a little bit of money, but they would never accept it from him. A church relief fund however, that was a different matter. It was not really a lie, out here in the countryside, he was the church.

To the left was the old widow Carbonari. He always visited on a Monday to read her the last rites. The widow Carbonari was not a hypochondriac. She knew she wasn't dying. She just liked having the last rites read to her. Every Monday morning Father Baggio would get a phone call telling him she was dying. He would pick up the flowers he'd bought the day before and dutifully visit in the afternoon. After a cup of tea and a chat she'd tell him she was feeling much better now. Father Baggio liked the widow Carbonari and dreaded the day that he wouldn't get the phone call saying she was dying.

Straight ahead at the crossroads was the city of Florence. Father Baggio decided to take the right turn. The widow Carbonari would still be there when he'd finished dispensing with his money. After all, she wasn't dying.

This was one of those significant days in Father Baggio's life. People highlight these days and use words like destiny and fate. Destiny usually refers to an apex of greatness in somebody's life. People connect the word destiny to a masterful deed and it's often seen in a glowing light of achievement; it was his or her destiny. However, anyone using the word destiny about their own life should be avoided at all costs, and definitely never given the power to rule a country. Fate on the other hand is often used in a more negative light. When something goes wrong fate is usually the one to get the blame. For some inexplicable reason people often need to label events under the guise of some all powerful omnipotent force that guides their actions. These people are wrong. Fate and destiny are merely bystanders watching the game of life and chuckling to themselves from a distance. It was not fate nor destiny that made Father Baggio turn right. Father Baggio chose to turn right. Fate was not the malevolent force in his decision it was choice, and in this case it was a bad choice.

Less than half a mile along the road Father Baggio came across two strangers hitching. Must be tourists he thought to himself. The road as he well knew led to a comparative nowhere. The only significant destinations were the farmstead of the family he was visiting and the old keep. The road ended just short of the wrought iron gates that marked the perimeter of the castle grounds. No-one ever gained access there. Father Baggio knew very little about the man who lived there. He never came into the small town and from what he had learnt over the years he worshipped another God; that of science. Baggio pulled up alongside and leant a friendly face out of the window.

'Are you looking for somewhere? I can give...' Father Baggio stopped abruptly. He still had the gift that he'd inherited from Nana Baggio. 'Oh sorry but...'

Iscyrus instantly recognised the signs of suspicion. He hadn't survived walking the Earth all these years without knowing when someone saw through his human guise. He'd also spent a considerable amount of time learning the best ways to kill and he had his favourite. Given the chance Iscyrus used the heart, it somehow seemed a fitting way for a Demon to kill. He liked to slice the aorta with his razor sharp stiletto knife. Granted it wasn't the most efficient way to kill, it took time for the heart to pump out the life giving blood, but he enjoyed the irony. The heart gave you life but it also took it away.

With the speed of a striking cobra on performance enhancing drugs Iscyrus struck. Shortly after Father Francesco Baggio became just another digit in a long number of casualties in the battle between good and evil.

Dr Laura Welsh watched as Iscyrus forced the body of the priest into the boot. Inside her a voice screamed out; *'this is wrong he was an innocent man, you didn't have to kill him!'* The voice quickly became muffled as her now almost entirely dominant side, Martha, forced the voice deeper into the recesses of her mind. That's the trouble with a good conscience; it's all too easy to silence with a metaphorical sock stuffed in its mouth, especially when a really good offer comes around. Granted it'll return when the dust has settled just to make you feel bad but by then it's too late.

'You're the sort that give hitchers a bad name,' chuckled Dr Welsh as they climbed into the front of the car.

'mmmm mmph mmm!' screamed her conscience, deep inside the recesses of her mind.

The drive to the perimeter gate of the keep didn't take long. Iscyrus loved hitching. Peoples' favoured choice of travel varies; some like trains, others like flying, for Iscyrus it was hitching. It was cheap, you got to meet new and interesting people, and there was always somewhere to dump the car afterwards. Dr Welsh stepped out and walked to the intercom system at the entrance gate.

'State your names and intentions please,' announced a voice through a crackling speaker.

'Dr Laura Welsh and Dr Wolfgang Hissel. Our intention is to find truth through the art of scientific discovery,' she responded in line with the preordained response to gain access into the Galileist headquarters.

'Then answer these three questions to prove your intellectual worth.'

'Malcolm do we have to go through this? Kloch is expecting us, you know who I am, you can see me on your monitor,' she looked up at a camera located just inside the fence and smiled as she spoke.

'But it's on the card. It's tradition, three questions. Anyway I don't know Dr Hissel nobody here has met him before.'

'He's here with me. He's our newest member and he is expected. Now open the gate Malcolm.'

'Just one question then, I'll make it easy. What is the

atomic number of Gallium?'

'31. Now open the bloody gate!'

'Okay but Professor Kloch will hear about this. The questions are there for a reason you know.'

'Yes and as you well know that reason is to keep even the most persistent door to door salesmen out.'

The gate made a clicking sound and slowly opened. Dr Welsh and Iscyrus entered and headed towards the keep. The extremely long driveway although relatively new, already showed signs of disrepair. Cracks had appeared and vegetation had sprung through the gaps in the block paving. The three gate questions had only ever failed once; Seamus O'Leary driveways.

Chapter 12

The duck approached the large yacht that had appeared without any reasonable warning in the lake where it lived. It hadn't paid attention to the other ducks that had flown away, wings flapping the agitated water in their haste to leave. This duck was extremely rare. Its rarity had little to do with its species, it had more to do with its personality. It was a curious duck. Any creature that so many predators find quite tasty and at the same time is extremely curious about things, is rare. The duck had two thoughts concerning the yacht; if it was edible and if it wanted to be friends. It gave a few pecks at the side of the boat; not edible. The sudden appearance of a man leaning over the side shouting at it, told the duck it wasn't friendly either. *Oh well* it thought as it paddled away.

'Did you just see that?' asked Norris in way of complaint. 'Just finished patching one hole in the hull and a flipping duck tries pecking another one.'

'A duck couldn't peck a hole through your yacht,' announced the Professor sagely.

'Why not? A woodpecker could. And they've both got beaks,' Norris leant back over the side. 'Vandal! Plum sauce! Hah! That's sent you packing hasn't it?'

Eleri looked up from her notepad.

'How do you spell delusional paranoia?'

Jenny sitting next to Eleri gave a chuckle.

'Come and sit down dear,' she said patting the seat next to her. 'We're about to plan our strategy.'

'Am I really being paranoid?' whispered Norris as he sat down.

'Well maybe a little bit.'

'See that's the problem with paranoia. You don't

know you're being paranoid until someone points it out. Even then you could be so paranoid that you don't trust them to be telling the truth about your paranoia. Although I suppose you could be paranoid about being paranoid, then you're deliberately looking out for the signs.'

Jenny gave a little giggle and intertwined her arm around his. Norris really was funny in a cute way. She couldn't imagine life without him anymore.

'Okay we're all here. I'll begin,' said Death.

'Er this is a committee meeting. Shouldn't we start with a role call?' interrupted Reg.

'It's not really a committee meeting Reg and I can see everyone's here. Oh wait where's Jenny? There she is,' said Death in his sarcastically laden tongue.

'Okay, okay. Shall I take the minutes?'

Death gave Reg a strained look.

'Well we might want to check the plan later. And I've got my black book. The one with the pencil in the binding.'

'Okay Reg you do that. Right first of all, it's obvious we're dealing with some serious people here. They've got a deadly plague in their possession and I don't think they're scared to use it. I've spoken to Michael and he says the cure is still some time off completion. So we're all at risk here.'

'Er. What do you mean all at risk? Surely it's only Norris, he's the only mortal isn't he?' asked Reg.

'This is a curse from God. Nobody is safe, it will effect all of us. With that in mind; anyone who wants to leave right now can do so. Just raise your hand and you can leave with no ill will from me. Norris that doesn't include you so put your hand down. It doesn't include you either Reg. Good so we're all decided. Comrades together huh Reg?'

'Yer,' mumbled Reg.

'Unfortunately we've had some bad news from the boffins back at the laboratory,' continued Death. 'The Eleventh Plague is an airborne depression and highly contagious. The original projection for suicide rates was underestimated. They hadn't taken into consideration that nobody would be able to comfort those suffering without getting it themselves. Without the comfort of others... well I'm sure you can work it out. But don't worry I'm sure we'll get to these Galileists before they release the plague, and when have I ever been wrong? Put your hand down Reg it was a rhetorical question.'

Eleri raised her hand. Death pointed to her to continue.

'Eleri Jones, Angelic Times...'

'This isn't a press call.'

'Yer but I thought you'd appreciate the atmosphere.'

'Ha ha.'

'We all know what's at stake. So what's the plan?'

'We're going to split up, into two groups.'

'Like they always seem to do in the films?'

'Yes.'

'When they end up getting picked off one by one?'

'Yes. I mean no,' Death took a deep breath before continuing. 'The Professor and I are going to try and get to the Galileists before they can release the plague. We're going to follow an ancient secret pathway laid down in a series of secret markers.'

'That sounds like a book I read. Where a professor did exactly that to find a secret sect that was against the church,' commented Eleri.

'Look this is my plan. I came up with it. I haven't just stolen the idea from a book. Talk like that could get me sued or something,' grumbled Death.

'I wasn't suggesting anything of the sort,' said Eleri with a smirk. 'Anyway I'm coming with you. Like I said before, this is my story and I'm not letting you out of my sight.'

'Okay,' sighed Death. 'The Professor, me and Eleri Jones are going to find the Galileists before...yes Reg?'

'If you're going after the Galileists shouldn't I come?' suggested Reg pulling his trousers up at the waistband. 'After all I'm a Vengeance Angel and there might be trouble.'

'You're not a qualified Vengeance Angel. You're on work experience.'

'Well I'm the closest thing you've got to a Vengeance Angel and I know some moves. I've battled demons before.'

'Yes and I was there,' said Death. 'And these moves, wouldn't happen to be *kick them in the shins* would they?'

'Well. Erm. Yes. But it's a tried and tested method. And I'm pretty damn sure those Galileists wouldn't like being kicked in the shins one little bit either!'

'Okay,' agreed a resigned Death. 'The Professor, me, Eleri Jones and Reginald the Vengeance Angel will track down the Galileists. The rest of you, which is now Jenny and Norris will go and meet the Galileist representative at the Bargello and do the trade.'

'Er, I didn't think there was a formula for life. How are we going to do the exchange?' asked Norris.

'Professor, the formula please.'

Professor Bostock stood up and took out an envelope from his inside pocket.

'I've created a formula for life,' he said holding up the envelope.

'Really?' asked Norris.

'No not really, but it should be a good enough fake to buy us some time if nothing else.'

'The plan is straightforward,' interrupted Death. 'Jenny and Norris will hand over the fake formula and fingers crossed it fools them, either enough for them to hand over the plague or at least to gain us some valuable time. Meanwhile, the rest of us will try to track them down.'

'What if you can't find the Galileists and they don't believe the fake formula? asked Norris.

'Then I suppose we'll have to try and force the information out of their representative, whoever that may be. The rest of us will try to join you at the Bargello, if we can't find the headquarters in time. If we don't get back in time, just follow them till we arrive. Whatever happens we can't fail at this. I really believe that they'll release the plague like they said. We're dealing with a pretty nasty terrorist organisation here, not just a bunch of geeky scientists.'

Chapter 13

The Galileist headquarters didn't really have security guards, it had a skinny scientist with a set of nunchucks stuffed into his oversized lab coat pocket. His name was Dr Malcolm Pendelbury. The Galileist Institute had employed security staff in the past, but found that the burly guards had bullied the scientists working there. Malcolm wasn't even officially employed as security, he was a research assistant; but he'd appeared to be the most qualified at the time to take over the extra duties as he had his very own set of nunchucks.

Malcolm had bought the nunchucks to protect himself, after one of the younger boys had stolen his scientific calculator when he was fifteen. He'd decided to teach himself how to use them and practised quite a lot in those early days. He soon learnt that the nunchucks were a very efficient weapon for causing harm. Unfortunately, he soon learnt from several nasty bumps and bruises, that the nunchucks caused harm to the one wielding them. Probably the best way to use them was to give them to your assailant and let them do the damage to themselves. Malcolm hadn't carried them for years, not since his mother had banned him practising when he broke her favourite lamp, but he carried them now. He was Chief Security Officer; just like Worf in Star Trek! He wasn't officially Chief Security Officer but he had the nunchucks!

The only other person in the security office was Dr Victoria Kloosterman. She was armed with a broken mop; an elastic band had been taped to the handle allowing her to attach it to her wrist and swing it around freely, thus enabling her to attack multiple enemies at once! Victoria was Malcolm's unofficial girlfriend. Unofficial in the sense that they hadn't been on any dates, hadn't kissed, and he'd only got as far as *will you gggargh* when asking her out. Although, they were lovers in the office's weekly *role playing game weekends*. She was the beautiful Elven warrior Princess Aissyia and he was Lord Vissek, a battle weary knight. She had charmed him with the Amulet of Eldoron. In the the real world the Amulet of Eldoron was replaced with a home-made cupcake she brought in for him whenever they worked together. She also knew a lot about particle accelerators which was pretty damn cool!

Malcolm watched as Dr Welsh and whom he believed to be Dr Hissel approach the front door of the Galileist Headquarters. The monitor in the security office flickered and he gave it a bang with a flat palm. It hadn't been the same since Dr Rykerman had rigged up all the monitors together for a mammoth game of Pac-Man. Malcolm picked up the phone next to the monitor.

Professor Maximillian Kloch let the phone ring three times before answering. He could have answered immediately. It only required the pressing of a button on the control pad situated on the arm of his motorised wheelchair. He liked to let it ring a few times though. It gave an appearance of normality, like he had to walk to the phone before answering.

'Dr Welsh and Dr Hissel have arrived sir.' Malcolm's voice resonated through the loudspeaker.

'Good send them down to me immediately.'

'Sir. I would just like to say that she refused to follow the entrance gate procedure. She wouldn't answer the three questions. Well it undermines my authority as Chief Security Officer. The questions are traditional and they're there for a reason.'

Yes thought Kloch they're there to keep door to door salesmen out.

'I'll have a word with her Malcolm.'

Maximillian Kloch pressed another button ending the conversation, ducked his head down, and let out a long deep breath. It was a sigh of relief, the plague had made it safely to the keep. In a few minutes Kloch would have the most destructive weapon available to mankind. If it had fallen into the wrong hands it would have been globally catastrophic. It was the one plague that had been deemed to be too harsh to use on the Ancient Egyptians and if the records were right they had been pretty naughty. Luckily, Maximillian Kloch head of the Galileists was a humanitarian. His middle name was philanthropy, well actually it was Algernon, but it didn't change his views. He had no intention of using the plague for any evil purpose. Purely and simply he wanted to find a cure. He wanted to send a message to God, and the usual line of communication, namely praying, didn't really suit his purpose. He wanted to show the Church that it was no longer needed. Science was here now and its presence was surplus to requirements. They say that revenge is a dish best served cold. Kloch was more the sort to serve it with a nice warm chocolate pudding to cushion the blow. Nevertheless it would be revenge.

It had been the chaplain at the hospital that had broken the news to him that his wife and unborn child had died in the crash. He had told him that sometimes there may seem no reason for these things, and that the Lord's ways were mysterious to man. That it was a miracle that he had survived and there was surely a purpose for his life. Kloch knew better. It was a genetic abnormality that had saved him. The shard had missed his heart by millimetres because his heart was a centimetre or so further to the right than it should have been. Science gave him the reason why he'd survived, not God.

Kloch pressed the short stubby stick that controlled his wheelchair and motored into his personal laboratory in the adjoining room. The other scientists referred to Kloch's residence as the dungeon. The name was apt; it was the old dungeon, although it barely resembled its medieval origins. The interior of Kloch's laboratory looked like something from a science fiction film, without the fiction and a bit more science. It was how a young child opening their first junior chemistry set imagines the contents of the box will transform their room. The laboratory would have satisfied even the wildest of imaginations, unlike the box that provided a handful of test tubes and a bunsen burner of sorts. Kloch's eyes were drawn to the large reinforced glass box. It was more like a small room than a box. It was where the plague would be housed. Two sets of black gloves were fitted into the side allowing the operative to work without contact. Although access into the sealed container was possible, mechanical arms and a series of conveyor belts were responsible for bringing the plague from the storage facility to the worktable near the gloves. Everything needed to experiment on the plague was on the inside and everything was linked to the computer on the outside. Kloch had designed it with safety in mind, there would be no need for any contact with the plague once it was inside the box. It was cutting edge stuff and definitely not the kind of thing you'd find in a junior chemistry set, even the deluxe edition.

Maximillian Kloch looked around the room with the pride of a new father. The Galileist Institute was his family and science was their home. Soon his Deputy Head would arrive with what would be their crowning glory. He'd had doubts about Dr Laura Welsh when she'd first approached the organisation. She was just too young to have achieved all that she had. Her rise in the scientific community had been meteoric. It was the kind of rise that made others suspicious that outside forces were helping her along the way. Dr Welsh had proved herself though. It was her genius that had given Kloch the original idea to steal the plague. She'd read his article on the proof of God and suggested the next logical step. Her involvement hadn't stopped there, she'd even helped him formulate a plan to obtain the plague. She'd provided practical and viable solutions to the problems that they'd faced every step along the way. He knew that the real work was only just about to begin. It would take months maybe even years to find a cure for the plague, but it still felt like this was a celebratory moment. As he returned to his office to meet Dr Welsh and Dr Hissel he looked up at the plaque above the laboratory door. *The Galileist Institute: For the betterment of Humanity.*

Malcolm slammed his hand against the side of the monitor. The screen was completely dead.

'Damn Dr Rykerman and his mammoth game of Pac-Man,' he cursed.

'Are we a little bit touchy because we were beaten by a girl?' teased Victoria.

'I was suffering from an acute bout of hay fever that day, as well you know. And no it's not that. How are we supposed to act as security if we can't watch the facility?' Malcolm reached for the phone. 'I'm going to call Kloch.' Malcolm slowly replaced the phone. 'The line is dead.'

Professor Cobblers worked for months on a thesis regarding the problem of a dead phone line. Under the title *the Unsolvable Dilemma* Cobblers proposed that there are problems in life that have no solution. As an example he stated that when your phone line is dead the only way to get it fixed is to phone the company to fix it. But your phone is dead so you can't phone them and so the problem proceeds in an endless cycle. One of his more reckless students then pointed out that this type of dilemma had already been identified in Joseph Heller's book *Catch 22*, thereby nulifying Professor Cobblers' work. The student is now facing his own *Catch 22*. How to avoid Professor Cobblers, who now wants to kill you, when the only way to avoid him is by leaving University and the only way to leave University is to pass Professor Cobblers' class. And that's *the Unsolvable Dilemma.*

'It's only a dead phone line, it's probably just a coincidence,' said Victoria responding to the worried expression on Malcolm's face.

'No it's really strange.'

'Nah. Dr Rykerman probably linked the closed circuit line to the phone line when he was messing around. Eat your cupcake, I'll check the phone lines in the rest of the building.'

'No don't open the door!'

Too late. Victoria clicked the button that released the door lock. The door burst inwards sending Victoria flying back into the room with a short scream. Malcolm looked into the eyes of Iscyrus. He was no longer Dr Wolfgang Hissel, the eyes that Malcolm saw did not hold a trace of humanity. There was no mercy in those eyes. With a slow deliberate movement Iscyrus drew out his stiletto knife. Malcolm reacted. Not as quickly or as efficiently as he would have liked but at least he reacted. Stumbling out of his chair he pushed Victoria behind him and fumbling pulled the nunchucks from his pocket. Despite the feeling of impending doom Malcolm still felt nervous about actually hitting someone. He'd only ever been in one fight before, and that only counted if you included holding your hands over your head and whimpering *please stop,* while being pummelled all over your body. That had worked out okay in the end though, Janet Morgan had ended up being a close friend.

Malcolm decided he'd intimidate the attacker with some of his more extravagant moves, then maybe he'd go away. Iscyrus watched; amusement playing on his lips as Malcolm swung the nunchucks around his body. Malcolm truly believed he was doing well, his arms flailing around his body, the nunchucks' clicking chain following the unorthodox rhythm. Rapidly growing in confidence he attempted one of his more deadly moves. It had been the one that had broken his mother's favourite lamp. He executed it, but not in the traditional, and most importantly successful sense. Malcolm's eyes glazed over as the hard wooden handle of his weapon struck the back of his head. Iscyrus watched as the body of the crumpled scientist fell to the floor. Then, his attention turned to Victoria.

With the eyes of Iscyrus upon her, Victoria became aware she wasn't an Elven warrior princess, and she wasn't actually holding a weapon capable of attacking multiple enemies at once. She was holding a broken mop with an elastic band taped to the handle. She dropped it to the floor.

'Well done,' said Dr Welsh giving a slow sarcastic clap as she entered the room. 'It would have been so inconvenient to have my colleague here kill you. They would have interviewed you straight after your death. And that would have led them here, to us.'

'Laura what's going on? I don't understand.' Victoria glanced from Dr Welsh to Iscyrus in quick succession.

'Oh Laura's not here. She's sleeping,' said Dr Welsh tapping the side of her head. 'You're talking to Martha now.'

Kloch was growing impatient. It wasn't the nurtured impatience of a long wait, it was the rapid growth impatience that springs up when you're desperate for something to happen.

'What's taking them so long?' he muttered under his breath.

As if to avoid any further questioning the lift sprang to life. Kloch turned his attention to the sound of mechanical whirring that emanated from its door.

The lift opened directly into his office, a necessary convenience for a man confined to a wheelchair.

'You did it. You've brought me the plague?'

Dr Laura Welsh stepped out of the elevator. 'Of course.'

'Let me see,' said Kloch eagerly, ignoring the second figure that stepped out behind Dr Welsh.

Dutifully Dr Welsh pulled the jar containing the plague from her bag. A slight panic crossed Kloch's face.

'It's in a jam jar!'

'It's not a jam jar, it has one of those child safety lids.'

'It's not safe in that! Quickly we must get it into the storage facility.'

Kloch spun his wheelchair around, indicating for them to follow him. He reached the computer terminal and tapped in a series of numbers, Dr Welsh close behind him. The entrance to the facility opened.

'Quickly get it inside.'

As soon as the plague was secure Kloch turned to Dr Hissel and held out his hand.

'Dr Wolfgang Hissel, welcome to the Galileist Institute. Sorry about that but do you have any idea what would have happened if that plague had leaked out from its container?'

'Oh yes,' interrupted Dr Welsh. 'Millions, perhaps billions of people would have died.'

Kloch looked at her face. He was surprised by her

sudden cold declaration. 'You gave the cure to Mangella for his daughter?'

'Do you know I completely forgot.'

'I worked on that for months. What's going on? What's the matter with you? Dr Hissel? Kloch turned from one to the other.

'Oh that isn't Dr Hissel. Let's just say Dr Hissel had a spot of misfortune. This is Iscyrus.'

'You will explain to me what is going on right now!'

'Of course, but first...' Dr Welsh walked to the back of the wheelchair and ripped out the power cable. 'We wouldn't want you running off from us now or should I say wheeling off. Oh and your phone line is dead too just in case you were wondering.'

'Explain yourself immediately!' commanded Kloch but his voice wavered with a nervous edge.

'Ah yes keep the crazed megalomanic talking, and while they explain their dastardly plot the hero makes his move and saves the day. We've all seen the films. Unfortunately for you Professor this is not the movies,' Dr Welsh looked down at the wheelchair. 'And I can't see you making any move soon. But I will explain our dastardly plot. It'll make this all the more sweeter. So why am I doing this? Simple. For the money. I am holding the world to ransom. They either pay or I release the plague. I know if I'd waited for the cure that would have brought wealth too, but to be honest I couldn't be bothered waiting.'

'This is some kind of joke. This is insane. Why come to me if you didn't want a cure?'

'Oh I still needed you. That facility in there. I needed somewhere to transfer the plague into its new container, the one with the bomb attached. Then there was your influence. I needed the Galileist Institute to entice Dr Wolfgang Hissel, he was such an admirer of your work. And finally and most importantly, I needed someone to take the blame. What use is a bank balance of a few billion pounds if everybody is after you? The Galileists, a secretive terrorist sect, full of evil scientists bent on the destruction of the Church, a perfect scapegoat don't you think.'

'You'll never get away with it!'

'Oh dear, we are full of clichés today, but then I suppose I do have my own. Goodbye Professor Kloch.'

Iscyrus stepped forward his knife in hand. Kloch raised his arms to protect himself, but Iscyrus knew exactly how to strike at an opponent. He threw a slight feint towards Kloch's face. Instinctively Kloch raised his arms. People always protect their face first, thought Iscyrus as he struck at the heart. The whole exchange had taken less than a second, Iscyrus removed the blade and joined Dr Welsh in the laboratory.

Chapter 14

Bacchaus sat at his ornately carved desk. Had he been human you would probably describe him as a bad man, a very bad man at that! Bacchaus however was not a human, he was a Demon and as such very bad becomes a pointless description. The phone on his desk rang. Bacchaus gave a crooked smile as he switched the loudspeaker on.

'Ah Iscyrus. I presume it is done?'

'It is.'

'And our sacrificial pawn?'

'Has no idea what's going on.'

'Excellent. I knew I could count on you my old friend.'

Bacchaus pressed the button to hang up the phone. With a slow deliberate movement he leant back into his chair, his plan for revenge was almost complete. A strange melancholy passed across his face. He was not prone to bouts of melancholy, and wistful thoughts barely entered the equation, but on this occasion he couldn't help but succumb. If only he could have been there to watch Kloch's face as he realised he'd been betrayed, to watch as his last breath left him. Oh how he missed the ability to walk the Earth amongst those pitiful humans. Those were the good old days before he'd been banished. A knock at the door broke his thoughts.

'Enter.'

Bugflug entered pushing the door open with his foot, his hands full of precariously balanced loose leafed documents. Bugflug stumbled his way over and unloaded the various documents onto the desk.

'Is something wrong Sire?' he asked noting the expression on Bacchaus' face.

'Ah I just miss the good times. Oh how I would've loved to have been up there today,' Bacchaus pointed upwards with his index finger.

It is a generally accepted fallacy that the realm of Hell is somehow to be found in the very depths of the Earth, although it is actually on a different plane of existence. Heaven is above and Hell is below have in fact become the generally acknowledged terminology, despite being wildly inaccurate both geographically and dimensionally. Most denizens of Hades know this, but still use terms like down below and the Underworld for convenience sake, it's just easier that way.

'What's brought this on sire?'

'It's a just silly little thing. An old colleague of mine shattered a man's dreams and then killed him today. He went into the man's office just at the moment he believed his dream was about to come true and killed him. Told him of his failure first of course. I just wish I could have been there to witness it. You know, the expression on the broken man's face, that sort of thing.'

'Maybe I could check if there's any CCTV footage Sire. Then you could watch the cruelty and violence in the comfort of your own home.'

'Yes, that would be nice,' sighed Bacchaus. 'Anyway back to work. What's on the agenda for today?'

'I've brought the updated plans for your private torture chamber and prison. They are waiting your approval. May I just point out a possible flaw though Sire?'

'Yes?'

'Someone appears to have connected a ventilation shaft to a prison cell corridor. This will surely present the opportunity for escape.'

'I don't think we need to worry about that. I designed it myself. Next?'

Bugflug quickly moved to the next document. 'I have a report here Sire.'

'I can see that.'

'Er, it's quite disturbing news. One of your subjects appears to have developed a nasty case of Christianity. Right here in Hell. Changed from a perfectly good Demonic name, Gunthra, to Samuel. Trouble is he's from a well respected family; the Baby Slaughterers from the Fourth Level of Hades. I think perhaps we should make a public spectacle of him, set the right example. No one above the rules, just because you're from an influential evil dynasty. Apparently this Christianity can spread quite quickly if it's not stopped early.'

'Leave that one to me.' Bacchaus took the report from Bugflug and placed it in the top drawer of his desk. 'Next?'

'Here's something that might cheer you up. The Torture Unit in the False Idol Worshipping Department have composed a choral piece in your honour. They've gathered up some sinners to perform it for you tonight.'

'Plenty of high notes?'

'Oh yes Sire. I've been informed that there are a multitude of impossibly high notes.'

Bacchaus' enjoyment of the impossibly high notes had little to do with the resonance of such notes, but more to do with how they were achieved. His particular favourite, the triple high c, is only achieved by thrusting white-hot sharp metal objects into the sensitive areas of a singer's anatomy.

'Oh good I do like the impossibly high notes. Anything else?'

'Just the usual punishments and tortures to sign off,' said Bugflug passing the pile of remaining documents across the desk. 'Oh and we're expecting an increased number of sinners over the next few days. It's freshers' week at the universities, so perhaps enlist in some extra Imps to help with the workload?'

'Yes indeed. If I can leave that with you?'

'Consider it done Sire.'

'Then you may go.'

Bugflug just reached the door when Bacchaus called him back.

'Oh Bugflug, just one thing.'

'Yes Sire?'

'I would like to commend you on your efficiency.'

'Thank you Sire.'

'But please try to do something wrong soon. I really do need a new pair of curtains.'

Chapter 15

Professor Guiseppe Caesaro sat on his sofa staring blankly at the three figures opposite him. The shock had informed his mind it should be elsewhere at this present time. His mind had taken the advice and had decided to visit his childhood. It was a safe place, full of sunny days, open fields and butterflies fluttering by. A short stubby man entered the room.

'There you go comrade, try this.'

Caesaro's hands automatically brought the cup to his lips and he took a sip. The strong sweet coffee informed his mind that the holiday was over and it was time to return to the present.

'So allow me to get this correct,' said Caesaro. 'You're Death? The Death?'

'That's right,' said Death. 'Not *the* Death though, I'm *a* Death. There are a lot of us. It's to do with the expanding population and all that, far too much work for one person. I'm Death number 221, Second Class, Head of Plagues.'

'So you're not a salesman then?'

'No.'

'It's just I thought. Well I imagined Death would be wearing a black cloak and carrying a scythe. You're wearing a suit. Although I might add it is a particularly fine example, who's your tailor?' Caesaro was Italian after all.

'Armando Vespucci from Magdalene Row,' said Death admiring the fine cut of his jacket. 'Obviously he only caters for the afterlife but I'll give you his number just in case. You never know.'

'So you are Death then?'

'Yep.'

'And you three are ghosts?'

'Actually I'm a Vengeance Angel,' said Reg.

'You're an Angel? Why haven't you got wings?'

'Well er, I'm not fully qualified yet.'

'Right okay, you're Death, you're an Angel and you two are ghosts.'

'Actually we're solid incarnations of our souls. But ghosts will do,' added Bostock after a stern look from Death.

'I'm supposed to believe this am I?' asked Caesaro incredulously.

'It's me, Professor Bostock. You know I'm dead. You went to my funeral.'

'Erm.'

'You did go to my funeral?'

'Well no. Sorry. There was a documentary on about secret sects within ancient Mayan culture.'

'Well the others did. We shared the same colleagues, they must have mentioned it.'

'Erm. The others didn't go either.'

'What! Nobody came to my funeral?'

'Old Professor Wiggins went.'

'So only Wiggins turned up to see my body laid to rest.'

'Erm. He didn't actually witness your burial. He just turned up to the buffet afterwards.'

'Well what did Wiggins have to say about it?' asked a slightly distressed Bostock.

'He was disappointed.'

'And so he should have been. A close colleague dying and nobody bothering to turn up!'

'Er, no. He said the sandwiches were slightly passed their best. A bit dry I think he said. You're wife was there though.'

'I have never been married!'

'Oh. Wiggins said she was there. Are you sure? He

said she was a short dumpy woman with matted hair and well, she smelt a bit.'

'I don't know anyone like that.'

'Actually come to think of it, he was a bit suspicious that she may have been a bag lady. You know a tramp of sorts.'

'Oh that's great. The only person that turns up to my funeral is some woman off the street.'

'Wiggins went.'

'He only went because there was free food, you know what Wiggins is like. My life's work. My lasting legacy. How am I remembered? A couple of crusty ham sandwiches passed their best.'

'And being married to a bag lady,' said Death. He couldn't resist the extra dig. It was the Professor after all.

Bostock dipped his head into his hands and gave a long groan.

'If it's any consolation comrade. Lots of people went to my funeral,' said Reg.

'Nice one Reg,' whispered Death patting him on the back.

'How is that a consolation?' said Bostock looking up.

'Well I wasn't a famous academic, and I didn't really achieve any great renown and people still turned up to my funeral. So it probably didn't have anything to do with your successful career, why they didn't turn up I mean. It...' Reg stopped talking for brief moment. 'I'm not helping am I?'

'You're doing great,' encouraged Death smirking.

Eleri gave Death a sharp jab in the ribs with her elbow. 'Stop it.'

It should be taken into account that the popularity of Reg's funeral did not reflect the popularity of Reg. The attendance had more to do with J.P Reynolds and Son, the firm where he used to work, giving their employees tuesday afternoon off so they could pay their respects. J.P Reynolds and Son felt duty bound to grant this concession, they were a family business after all. Family business is usually a term used to conjure up an impression of a caring, friendly company, in order to entice customers to buy their products and to make employees feel looked after. In the Reynolds' case it was a family of selfish, uncaring and savagely ruthless capitalists. They had been extremely reluctant to give the afternoon off. They didn't want to set a precedent or employees would be dying all the time. However, Porchia Reynolds, the youngest daughter, had pointed out they didn't actually have to pay their workforce under contract and could make them work twice as hard for the remainder of the week to make up for lost time. J.P Reynolds and Son were a family business. They always thought of their employees first.

With the promise of an afternoon off work and various food stuffs stuck on little wooden sticks in the buffet afterwards, few could resist. There was even a large cake that everyone thought was a bit too much like a birthday cake to be appropriate, but that didn't stop everyone from having a slice, in remembrance of Reg of course.

'Okay shall we move on from all this talk of funerals,' said Death, the conversation was starting to remind him of work. 'Let's just forget about who we actually are, and just say we're a group of people interested in the Galileists. What can you tell us?'

A twinkle of academic fervour entered the dark brown eyes of Caesaro. As an old academic Caesaro enjoyed nothing more than telling people what he knew. Unfortunately he'd picked a subject that nobody really wanted to know about. For years he'd tried to corner people in parties to tell them about his work and for years people had suddenly realised their drink was empty, they needed the bathroom, or just plain needed to be somewhere else. His work had received a brief amount of interest when *that* book came out. Suddenly everyone wanted to know about secret codes and sects attached to famous historical figures, but it was short lived. Caesaro sprung up from his seat; an action that seemed far too sprightly for someone of his advancing years, but he didn't want to miss this opportunity.

'Into my study. Follow me,' said Caesaro leading the way.

The study looked like a library. Unfortunately it looked liked a library that had been struck by an F5 tornado and had subsequently replaced the Dewey Decimal system of filing with one that revolved around the premise of; *don't touch anything, I like it like this, I know where everything belongs.* There were almost certainly some chairs in there, but sitting would require the use of a digger and some serious excavation work. Around the room piles of papers were stacked high, tilting so precariously they made the Leaning Tower of Pisa look structurally sound. There was the distinct possibility that should a butterfly flap its wings on the other side of the world it would cause an avalanche of academic documents.

Philosophers are always warning of the destructive powers of the butterfly. They claim that their apparent benign existence is responsible for natural disasters throughout the planet, causing the deaths of thousands with the mere flap of their wings. However, what the butterfly has ever done to deserve such animosity within the philosophical community still remains a mystery.

Professor Caesaro waited while the others found a space amongst the books, documents and various papers lying scattered around the room. 'So tell me, what is it that you would like to know about the Galileists?'

'Bostock here told us you know of a secret and ancient path that leads, I mean led, to the Galileists' headquarters,' said Death standing on one foot. He wasn't too sure where he could actually place the other one.

'Ah yes. More a series of markers than a path. I believe you're referring to the *Solaris Linearis*; the line of the sun. You wish to find the markers?'

'Yes, definitely.'

'Well you've come to the right place. I'm the leading authority you know.' Professor Caesaro wasn't lying, he was the only authority.

'Good then you can help?'

'Yes indeed my dear fellow. But first you will need a bit of background knowledge,' Caesaro wasn't going to give up his chance of an audience that quickly.

'If we must,' grumbled Bostock. He'd been to enough parties with Caesaro to know the score.

Caesaro ignored the comment. He'd been to enough parties to know to carry on regardless while he still had the chance.

'The Galileists were formed in 1693 by Vincenzo Viviani a former pupil and self styled last disciple of Galileo. Of course, back then they never referred to themselves as Galileists, that name only arose some years later. They originally called themselves *the starry messengers* after Galileo's published work *Sidereus Nucius* where he identified the four moons of Jupiter. Since Galileo's death Viviani had long campaigned for a fitting tribute in the form of a sepulchre, but he'd always been blocked by the Church. Galileo of course was found by the inquisition as *being subject to suspicion of heresy.*'

Death was suddenly very grateful that he'd never

been to a party with Caesaro.

'Erm, the Galileists?' prompted Death.

'Ah yes of course. It's all linked you see,' explained Caesaro. 'In 1693 Viviani received a worrying report from the Jesuit Antonio Baldigiani that the church was becoming increasingly hostile to mathematicians and physico-mathematicians. They were preparing a list of banned authors, Galileo amongst them. It was at this point I believe, that Viviani decided to form a secret sect away from the prying eyes of the Church. And this is where it gets interesting.'

Death had serious doubts whether Caesaro actually knew the definition of interesting, but allowed him to continue uninterrupted. He didn't really have a choice if he wanted to know about the Galileists' headquarters.

'A short while afterwards Viviani published an unremarkable book, it was basically a simple rehash of previous works and yet some of the great men of science at the time apparently held it in great esteem. I have a copy here,' Caesaro pulled out a small booklet from the shelf behind him. Look at the writing in the margin next to the diagram of the *Sala Meridiana*.'

Those who seek enlightened truth,
Beneath Medici's stars.
Solarus does the line provide,
And time does show the path.

Death read the line out loud. 'It's in English?'

'English was the language of science at this time,' explained Bostock.

'And of course English was the perfect language to hide something from the Church who considered it the language of barbarians and as such hadn't adopted its usage,' added Caesaro.

'Not much of a poem is it,' commented Reg.

'Viviani was a scientist not a poet,' said Caesaro. 'This is not an exercise in poetical verse, it is the *Solaris Linearis*. It was the key to finding the Galileist's meeting place.'

'What I'd like to know is why do these ancient secret sects always give these cryptic clues. Why don't they just say we're meeting at the Village Hall at 7.30?'

'It's so the Church won't find them.'

'But surely the Church could've solved the puzzle just like anyone else?'

'Ah now you might have a point there. Now this is interesting.'

Death gave Reg a nudge in the ribs. 'Stop asking questions.'

The others also gave Reg a disapproving look. He was like the classmate who insists on asking the teacher a question just as the bell for lunch rings.

'The Church may well have infiltrated the Galileists. Nicolas Fatio de Dullier was a Genevan mathematician and a very close friend of Isaac Newton. In 1693, the year the Galileist's were formed remember, Newton and Dullier had a well publicised failing out. Newton was documented to have had a nervous breakdown at the same time and wrote a letter to the diarist Samuel Pepys declaring he no longer wanted to see any of his friends. He certainly became very paranoid over whom he associated with. '

'Sounds like something from a seventeenth century gossip magazine,' said Death.

'Quite so. The thing is, clear lines were being drawn between science and religion at this time. And Dullier is documented to have joined a religious sect around the year of 1693. It is quite probable that Newton and Dullier fell out over the Galileist movement. Dullier could have been a spy for the Clergy!'

'So the cryptic clues were pointless. They just could

have said Village Hall 7.30!' said Reg triumphantly.

'Can we get back to the *Solaris Linearis*? asked Death.

'Oh yes of course, where was I?' Ah yes, the *Solaris Linearis*, the line of the sun, was the key. It told like-minded individuals where the Galileists were. In the same year...'

'1693,' sighed Death.

'Yes. A number of artistic and architectural tributes to Galileo began to spring up all over Florence. They were markers if you like, to lead you to the Galileists!' Caesaro stopped and looked around at his audience, either for applause or more likely as he suspected an excuse to leave. 'Doesn't anyone want to go to the toilet?'

'Er, no,' said Death. 'So why Florence?'

'It's in the *Solaris linearis*. Beneath the Medici's Stars. It's a double reference. Pointing to Galileo, he named the four moons of Jupiter the Medician Stars, after his Medici patrons. The Medici family created the Florence you see today. They were extremely generous patrons of the arts and science. Ergo anyone living at the time would immediately associate the name Medici with Florence.'

'So where can we find these markers?'

'To the best of my knowledge only two remain. The one is the facade on the Palazzo dei Cartelloni on Via Sant Antonino and the other is the fresco by Anton Domenico Gabbiani in the Pitti Palace.'

'That's where we need to go then. Eleri could you write down the *Solaris Linearis*? We can solve the clues as we go along.'

Eleri pulled out her notepad and quickly jotted down the cryptic poem.

'Your handwriting is terrible,' said Death looking over her shoulder. 'How are we supposed to read that?'

'It's shorthand! I'm sure that your secretary Miss

Holloway uses the same thing.'

'Erm, well no actually. I had a choice, someone with secretarial skills like typing and shorthand or someone with nice legs. I went with the legs.'

'That's sexist.'

'No it's not. I'd say Reg had nice legs if it was true.'

'I'll have you know there's nothing wrong with my legs,' said Reg. 'They reach the floor, what more do you want?'

'Well it's not very far for them to go is it,' pointed out Death.

'Oh another interesting thing...' Caesaro began.

'I think we've got enough interesting things to be going on with,' said Death with a straight face.

'Are you sure? This is a particularly interesting fact.' Caesaro was keen not to let such a captive audience go. Nobody had even excused themselves to go to the toilet yet.

'I'm afraid we must be getting on.'

Caesaro reached into a drawer and pulled out a bound journal.

'Well take this with you. It's a copy of an article I wrote on the facade at Palazzo dei Cartelloni. It will most certainly be of interest to you. And here...' he quickly wrote his number across the top. 'If you have any questions I'd be glad to be of assistance. Any questions about this at all. Maybe one or two questions you might have now?' asked Caesaro hopefully as his guests began to leave.

'Thank you for your help Professor Caesaro,' said Death as they made their way out the front door.

'It was a pleasure and please don't forget to ask if you have anymore enquires.'

'Goodbye.'

'Or is it *au revoir*?'

'No I think goodbye will do.'

The casual observer may have viewed Death's insistence of using goodbye as slightly abrupt and unnecessarily harsh. To many the word goodbye is just a polite way of informing others that you no longer want to talk to them anymore. In many ways similar to *bugger off,* but used when there is a distinct chance of seeing that person again and not wanting to get a punch in the eye. For Death however, considering his role in society, it is far nicer to say goodbye than I'll see you again.

Chapter 16

Jenny sat alone on the yacht, brushing her hair in the mirror. That was the trouble with saving the world, your hair always got so tangled. The others had left Norris and her to make the exchange at the Bargello tomorrow at noon whilst they went to see Professor Caesaro and hopefully track down the Galileists. It was the first time in weeks that they had been able to spend some quality time together... alone. So it had come as quite a surprise that Norris had suddenly decided that he'd needed to pop out a minute. When she'd pressed him why he had to pop out, he'd simply said he needed to get some cigarettes. Norris didn't smoke. Norris was not a good liar. Luckily, Jenny knew she could trust Norris implicitly, which was rare even amongst Angels. That was what made Norris so special to her; he'd never do anything behind her back. Norris had lied to her but Jenny knew it could only mean one thing; he was planning a surprise for her. That was about as deceitful as he got, sneaking off to give her a surprise treat. She smiled to herself as she thought how lucky she was to have him.

Norris walked along the softly lit city streets of Florence. Although narrow in parts he didn't feel any threat from the darker corners created by the dim lighting. The air was full of light music, chatter and laughter, which wafted from the relaxed restaurants that dominated this part of the city. Norris did have a surprise for Jenny. Although he wasn't sure if it was a treat. He was going to ask her to marry him. Definitely this time. He was fairly sure this would be a treat, but not positive. Italian phrase book in hand, he visited various restaurants looking for the perfect one. Unfortunately, the few that he had visited so far, and that had appeared to be conducive, were too busy to fully accommodate seven hundred and thirty timid evangelists at table two. (It should be noted at this point that it is inadvisable to buy a cheap Italian phrase book from a guy with an east European accent who is standing on a nearby street corner). As Norris wandered to the next restaurant he contemplated the rise in global population, where you couldn't even book a table midweek. He figured that if it carried on like this the only shops left would have to be restaurants in order to cater for the increased population's need for a table for two on busy midweek evenings.

Norris was not alone in his contemplation of the rise in global population. A recent branch in theology has also taken to considering this problem, if indeed that is what it is; they're not decided yet. Demographic Theology has produced many differing thoughts on mankind's expansion, and is one of the most contested academic fields at present. Some argue that it is the Catholic church's steadfast condemnation of birth control that has created this phenomenon. Whilst the Catholic demographic theologians claim it is due to all the sex before marriage that is going on. Others blame science for prolonging life in general. The Jehovah Witness demographic theologians argue that it doesn't really matter as to why, but as to who goes to Heaven, because there's only so much space there.

As a side note it is worth mentioning that the Jehovah Witnesses' belief that Heaven is confined to strict size dimensions and can only allow a limited number of people in, has led to the creation of a special section in Heaven. It was decided that they should have their own space away from everyone else. This was to avoid them getting upset that they spent their whole lives pointlessly waking up angry people, who always seemed to have something better to do than stand on their doorstep chatting about God.

Perhaps the most controversial argument was presented by Dr Peter Hodgeson who with a small group of devout followers formed the Apologetic demographic theologians. The Apologists claim that God is in fact fallible and has made a number of crucial errors. As evidence they claim that God created too much water when he made the world. If he had just added a bit more land then the increased population would not be such a problem. The other demographic theologians universally condemned this theory and told the Apologists to *bugger off and set up their own branch of theology; Marine Theology*.

Luckily for Norris he was able to get a table at the next restaurant he came to, so he didn't have to worry about the population increase any longer. It was not because the next restaurant he entered wasn't too busy to fully accommodate seven hundred and thirty timid evangelists at table two, it had more to do with the fact that the owner didn't speak perfect English. That is to say that as tradition holds, perfect English is spoken by the Queen and he didn't sound like the Queen. However, his English was good enough to establish Norris' needs. It was of a standard that one would expect from an Italian man who had spent his formative years dating a girl from Ipswich. He hadn't dated a girl from Ipswich, but that was the standard of his English.

Norris was extremely happy with his choice. It looked exactly as he'd imagined a posh restaurant in Florence should look. His basis for how it should look was informed to a large degree by Pepe's; the Italian pizzeria on the high street where he used to live. The others that he'd previously visited didn't have the charm that this one did. He gazed at the atmospheric setting. The tables were adorned with red and white checkered cloth each holding a candle placed artfully in a raffia wrapped bulbous wine bottle. Light-hearted and upbeat instrumental music tinkled and crackled through speakers hidden in the various shrubbery pots dotted around the main dining area. It was the kind of music you would expect to hear at the wedding of a mafioso's eldest daughter, where the reception is packed with guests dancing frivolously around chairs. Those weddings are always busy because an invite is an offer you can't refuse. The walls were decorated with pictures of famous Italian singers and movie stars, (if you were Italian), and topped with a long line of bunting in the colours of the Italian flag. It was all brought together by a soft orange lighting that added to the romantic charm and hid the more dishevelled parts of the interior.

Norris phoned Jenny to tell her he was taking her out to a posh restaurant and to meet him there. He'd decided it would be easier to meet her than traipse back to the boat and get her, besides he needed a drink. He was going to ask the girl of his dreams to marry him and as such alcohol was required. An act that is commonly referred to as *Dutch courage,* although why the Dutch in particular should require alcohol to make them brave Norris had no idea.

At the bar, drink in hand Norris attempted to make small talk with the young waitress serving. It was a bold endeavour considering the following facts: Norris did not speak Italian. The waitress did not speak English other than yes; which in itself was a slight stretch on the term speak as it was more a smiling nod than an actual yes. Bizarrely the only other English she knew was *sorry I need to go and get a ratchet.* This may at first glance appear to be a relatively useless phrase to know but it's surprising how often it comes in handy. The final hindrance in Norris' attempts to make small talk was that he didn't have anything small to talk about. However, Norris was not the sort to let such factors get in the way, (he'd battled with incompetence most of his life) and phrase book at the ready launched into what might be deemed as large talk. The waitress later told her friends about the conversation and this is how she translated it:

'Hello Norris is me.'

'Yes.' (smile and nod).

'I'm wanting to marry.'

'Yes.' Albeit a bit nervously.

'I see a girl in here and hope she will be want to marry me.'

'Yes.' Nervously.

'So what thinks you about such an offer?'

'Er.' Very nervously.

'I have ring.' At this point in the conversation Norris held his grandmother's wedding ring out in front of him. 'What do you thinks?'

'Sorry I need to go and get a ratchet.'

(Later when Jenny had arrived she tried to warn her about the man she was with; he'd already proposed marriage to her behind Jenny's back. Jenny was left confused as to why this waitress had such an obsession with ratchets).

Interestingly *will you marry me* is one of the two hundred and fifty two phrases used by Italian men when requesting sex. It is often regarded as a successful ploy. However, it is rarely used as it can lead to a life without the very thing being asked for.

The English speaking owner reappeared, although his new official capacity was now that of *maitre d',* and showed Norris to his table. In an ingenious use of space

Norris' table was situated in an area that the normal rules of physics would not ordinarily allow it to be. To say it was cramped would not do justice to the flagrant abuse of the rules that govern relative space, mass and dimensions. The owner prided himself on fitting people in. It was a family tradition that had been passed down through the generations and with it came a mantra: There is always room for people with money. It had started over two millennia ago when his distant relative had been an innkeeper. He had turned down a young couple *with child on the way. There is no room at the inn* had been his response to their request. His nearest rival in the inn-keeping business had then offered them room in the stable and they accepted! Not only that, before the end of the night the stable had become full of customers; a whole bunch of shepherds and three wise and obviously rich men, who brought with them gold, frankincense and something called myrrh. The profit that his rival made that night allowed him to expand and eventually put all the other innkeepers in the vicinity out of business. It was a lesson in economics that is taught to young children throughout the Christian world; there is always room for people with money, especially during the busy Christmas period.

Jenny checked her appearance in the mirror, or specifically her new dress. It had been an extravagant purchase on her last shopping trip to the Joan of Arc Boulevard back home in Heaven. Norris hadn't seen it yet. She hadn't hidden it from him; Norris never complained when she bought things for herself. Her guilt over the purchase had more to do with her frugal nature as an Angel. Nevertheless she did love it. She would never have picked it out herself, but her friend Angel Lucy had insisted she try it on. Lucy was right. The cut was perfect for her, the slim shoulder straps highlighted her smooth décolleté and long slender neck. Its loose and lightly flowing knee length exaggerated every slight movement of her hips. And pale green, she never would have chosen pale green but it really did suit her. Jenny tightened the clasp of her single pearl necklace. She had worn that necklace the first time they'd gone on a date and to her it somehow represented their love. She looked at the mirror again and gave a slight giggle and a jig. One last thing. Norris had phoned saying he was taking her out to a posh restaurant and that could only mean one thing... they were going bowling! Reaching under the bed she pulled out her favourite bowling shoes and placed them in her bag.

As Jenny made her way to the restaurant she caught the eye of almost everyone she passed. Although her swaying dress made little in the way of noise everyone heard the sound of a gentle *swish* as she passed. She didn't notice the way she captivated and enchanted those she passed. If she had, she would have believed it was the dress, but it was so much more than the dress. It doesn't matter how exquisite a frame you put on a Renoir painting, people will always see the beauty of the painting not the frame. It wasn't merely physical appearance that entranced; her beauty went deeper, somehow when you looked upon Jenny you gazed into her very soul. It was as if the Renoir painting had suddenly developed a great personality.

Norris was an extremely lucky man to have Jenny. Actually he wasn't extremely lucky. It was just that he'd used all his luck up being with Jenny. Everything else that luck could grant him was denied. It didn't matter. As long as he had Jenny his life was perfect and he knew it. She was too good for him and that was the problem. Norris was about to ask her to marry him. It always seemed so easy in the films. Some clever little speech, some romantic setting, and if you wanted to add that surprise element the ring hidden somewhere;

inside the bottom of a champagne glass or in a cake, something like that. Norris thought about placing the ring in the dessert cake but wasn't really sure which cake she'd choose. It would involve chocolate that much was a given but beyond that he didn't really know. Besides it would involve the kitchen staff knowing and he wasn't sure she'd actually say yes. Come to think of it he wasn't entirely sure that Angels were allowed to marry, even other Angels, let alone mortals.

Norris took a deep breath to calm himself down. He needed to concentrate on his speech, he hadn't really thought it through. He knew the sentence *will you marry me?* had to go in there somewhere, but it usually needed a bit more than just blurting that out. Something about how special she was. The word angel was out. Most people got to use angel as a way of describing their love in a flattering light. As far as Jenny was concerned it was just a statement of fact and not very romantic because of it. Maybe he should start with what she meant to him. She was his north, his south, his east, his west, his working week and his sunday best. No wait, someone had already used that. Damn you Auden! How about *you to me are everything?* Damn! *The sweetest song that I could sing, ooh baby.* Already used. That was the problem, there were just too many films, songs and poems out there. Avoiding clichés was an almost impossible task. He couldn't even compare her to a summer's day. What made it even harder was that she *was* everything to him. There was nothing in his life that even came close to how important Jenny was to him. Certainly not sweet songs, summer days, or points on a compass. Without her he was empty husk, a spectator watching life move around him. Hey, actually, that was pretty good, maybe he could use that.

'Hey,' said Jenny tapping Norris on the shoulder and taking her seat opposite.

Norris quickly knocked over an empty wine glass as a traditional way of showing his surprise at her arrival.

'Surprised to see me or were you expecting someone else?' remarked Jenny giggling at Norris' attempts to straighten the fallen glass by knocking a fork off the table.

'Jenny.'

'Yes?'

'You mean more to me than cheesy pop songs and compasses.'

'Glad to hear it.'

'Oh and summer days. And winter ones too. All different types of day no matter what the weather.'

'Er thank you.'

'You're an angel.'

'Yes I am.'

'What I'm trying to say is that when you're not around I look at things. Erm, living things that move about.'

'Are you okay? Everyone seems to be acting awfully strange. The waitress kept pointing at you, saying she needed to get a ratchet.'

'I'm fine. It's just...' Norris suddenly realised he should be on one knee.

With a quick chair scraping scramble Norris jammed himself on the floor between the table and the wall. Positioning his body at a peculiar angle to enable him to fit in the limited space, Norris began again.

'I was wondering if...aghh.'

He suddenly broke off his attempt as his balance deserted him, quickly reaching out he pulled at the table cloth sending more cutlery to the floor and tipping over the wine glasses. Norris regained his balance firmly placing his left hand palm down on the floor and leaving his right hand raised above his head. The overall effect looked more like a decrepit crouch than a romantic down on one knee gesture; things were not going well. Whether things are going well is often determined by the individual's point of view, but even with the lowest expectations it was apparent that things were not going well. Norris didn't know how long he could hold his romantic position so he rejected the romantic speech approach and opted for the *just blurt it out* technique.

'Jenny, will you m...'

'Can I be of assistance sir?' asked the owner come *maitre d'* and now in his new official capacity head waiter.

'Er, yes,' said Norris standing up and brushing off his knees. 'Can we have a menu please.'

'They appear to be on the floor sir,' said the head waiter picking up the menus along with the spilled cutlery. One of the main advantages of being the head waiter was being able to delegate problem customers to other members of staff. 'I'll send your waiter over sir.'

'You were saying something?' asked Jenny as the head waiter left.

Norris had enough experience with things going badly to know that it was time to give up on the marriage proposal. To use the nautical term it was time to abandon ship.

'Doesn't matter.'

'No what is it? Is something wrong?'

'No. I was just going to say Jenny will you m...mm.' Think quick. 'M... mind if I order for both of us?' Perfect. It began with m and made him sound masterful. Norris always wanted to sound masterful and ordering for both of them showed that he could be. Just like James Bond. Although of course he'd always ask Jenny first before being masterful.

'No of course not.' Jenny always loved it when Norris tried to be masterful because quite simply he wasn't and it always made him sound cute. Especially when he asked for permission first.

The waiter arrived promptly. A bit too promptly if the truth be told. Norris had barely opened the menu.

'Ciao Signore. Sei pronto a ordinare?'

'Si.'

Norris knew that you should never send a waiter away no matter how early they turn up to take your order. If you send them away they will disappear for at least half an hour after you're actually ready to order to punish you for your indecision. Norris quickly ran his finger down the menu and made his choice.

'Polo e salca de fungee. E bustickets al peepee,' ordered Norris with the confidence of someone who may have just requested a large whale carcass marinaded in a fine leafy gutter sauce. 'Didn't know I could speak a little bit of Italian did you?' he said turning to Jenny.

'No. I don't think the waiter does either.'

The waiter stood still, his pencil poised to write anything that he considered sensible. In reality he knew exactly what Norris was trying to order but he had trained as a waiter in France, so instead he just stood there practising his bewildered look. Faced with the waiter's lack of response, Norris resorted to the age old method of point at the menu.

'Ah. Pollo e salsa di funghi. E bistecca e salsa pepe,' said the waiter knowingly. 'What an excellent choice sir,' he continued in perfect English adding insult to injury. He was trained in France after all.

'What did you order for me?' asked Jenny.

'Erm. It's a surprise.'

'Ooh. Is it?'

'Yes it is.' Norris wasn't lying.

It wasn't long before the food arrived. Far too quickly to have been cooked properly in Norris' opinion.

'You ordered me chicken and mushroom. It's perfect!

You always get everything right,' said Jenny as the plate was placed in front of her. 'How did you know that's exactly what I wanted?'

At this point Norris was tempted to say it's because I pay attention to you and we're soul mates. But due to his blundering order he decided it would sound a bit too much like a lie. He felt it was better just to smile mysteriously and give a confident shrug.

The waiter returned just as Norris stuffed a large portion of food into his mouth.

'Is everything to your satisfaction sir?'

'Chyes chankyou chou, chis chovely,' Norris replied, avoiding choking on his mouthful of steak by the narrowest of margins.

Whether he replied in Italian or English was almost impossible to tell, but the waiter seemed to take the response as a positive one. Although, even if Norris had tried to inform him that it tasted like the undercooked arse end of a dead rhino, the waiter would have interpreted it as very nice thank you. He had received the rigorous training of a French waiter. In compliance with strict guidelines he had waited until Norris' mouth was completely full before asking, thereby avoiding any unnecessary complaints. It may come as a bit of a shock to realise that French waiters learn anything more than how to be arrogant, but that would be a highly cynical viewpoint.

With all possibility of a marriage proposal long since extinguished, Norris surreptitiously slipped the ring back into his inside jacket pocket. Over recent months he'd taken to wearing white linen. It sort of went with the whole deep sea treasure hunter image; white linen trousers, white linen shirt and a pair of deckshoes. He was glad he'd worn his suit today, the inside pocket gave him somewhere safe to put his grandmother's ring. That was the problem with the white linen look, not enough suitable pockets for your valuables. Yes it looked great walking along deserted beaches like some romantic buccaneer, but there just wasn't anywhere to put your keys or for that matter your grandmother's wedding ring.

As he placed the ring safely in his pocket Norris pondered over an earlier conversation with Reg, when he'd confided in him about his intentions. To his surprise Reg said he'd once asked someone to marry him, when he was still alive. Naturally the girl, Tracy, had said no he explained without a trace of false modesty. What made it a particularly unsuccessful marriage proposal was the fact that she dumped him a week later. He had wanted to get married, she had wanted to get involved with a fireman called Terry. It did little to improve Norris' confidence, not that Jenny knew anyone called Terry, fireman or not.

With his indelible style Reg had not left it there. After viewing Norris' grandmother's ring he questioned why the middle class bourgeoisie found it so romantic to use the ring prised from the finger of a dead person. Certainly Tracy would have gone absolutely mad if he'd tried to pass on a second hand ring. Ain't I good enough for something new?, she would have complained. Norris was quite sure Jenny would see it differently. At that point the conversation had rapidly deteriorated into one of Reg's rants about the ideological divide between the working and middle classes.

'What are you thinking about?' Jenny asked breaking Norris from his thoughts.

'Taking jewellery from dead people.'

Chapter 17

Being lost is all about perspective. It is generally perceived that knowledge of your immediate vicinity in comparison to your surrounding area is an indicator of your lost status. As such, being lost can be ranked in a scale. Not knowing what street you are in - slightly lost. Not knowing what city you are in - pretty lost. Not knowing what country you are in - lost. Not knowing what continent you are in - very lost or very drunk; both equate to roughly the same level of difficulty in returning home and the exorbitant taxi fare that will be incurred on said journey. The trouble is that very few people can accurately pinpoint the location of Earth in the vastness of the Universe. Given a map of the Universe few could even correctly identify the location of our Galaxy to within a couple of billion light-years. In comparative terms getting lost anywhere on this planet is similar to getting lost somewhere between the sofa and the tv remote. Embarrassingly, in terms of the universe the vast majority of us are in fact extremely lost. This goes a long way to explaining the confused and bewildered nature of the human race, but seeing as we don't have anywhere particularly pressing to be, we may as well just try and enjoy the scenery until we see somewhere do recognise.

'For the umpteenth time, I know exactly where we are. We're not lost!' Death was exasperated. Reg had insisted on buying a map of the city and kept stopping every two minutes to consult it.

'Well I don't know where we'd be without this map,' said Reg.

Death opened his mouth and then closed it again. It was one of those statements that you really want to comment on but just can't find the right words to do it. He looked across towards Eleri and Bostock. From their faces he could tell they felt the same way.

'Right,' continued Reg, his index finger following the line of the map. 'We follow this road, and cross this bridge. Erm.' He leant his head closer to the map. The early morning sun had cast a shadow from the crease in the map across the words. 'The Pontchio.'

'It's the Ponte Vecchio.'

Reg flattened the crease. 'Oh yer. The Ponte Vecchio.'

'We're not taking the Ponte Vecchio.'

'Yes we should, look. It's the shortest route to the facade.'

'The Ponte Vecchio gets too crowded. It'll take forever to cross. Trust me, it's much quicker to take the slight detour and cross at the Ponte Santa Trinita.'

'Where?' Reg asked studying the map.

'Follow the crease. The Pontnita.'

Death was right. The Ponte Vecchio, the world renowned shop lined bridge, has long since been overcome by the burden of the holidaymaker. Once famous for the work of master craftsman and artisans the bridge has more recently become famous for the kind of tat that the Blackpool tourist industry thrives upon. Every spare inch of the bridge is taken up with street hawkers attempting to sell their wares to people who will be far too distant to complain after the two weeks it takes for the fine jewellery purchased to turn green. The space in-between those spare inches is filled with soon to be duped tourists. The most remarkable thing about the bridge in modern times is that it still somehow manages to bear the weight of so many fake designer handbags and sunglasses without collapsing into the Arno. This phenomenon has in itself given birth to its own tourist industry. It is *a must see* for any travelling economists as it's perhaps one of the finest examples of Congestion Economics in Europe.

Congestion Economics was first advocated by William Hershel III in his book *How I made a lot of money: From rags to a nice semi-detached house.* Hershel first realised the potential of Congestion Economics when he was still referred to as Wino Bill Hiccup. Since his first book Hershel has gone on to be a multi millionaire, and even owns his own vineyard, producing wine under the label Tramp's Choice; a fine white wine with a distinctive paint stripper flavour. His success story began when his main source of income was washing car windscreens at a set of traffic lights in Philadelphia. One fateful day he realised that it was far easier to make money when the traffic lights were red. If your potential customer was staying still there was an almost ninety five percent greater chance of gaining financial reward. Therefore it is reasonable to assume that the slower a customer moves the more money can be made. Congestion Economics is now one of the most widely used approaches in the retail sector as other businesses soon adopted the Hershel Approach. It is no coincidence that the majority of people work nine till five thereby ensuring that they all have to do their shopping at the same time. This leads to busy and congested shops and slower movement equals more money. Congestion Economics is perhaps most evident in the supermarket environment, where there are never enough till operatives. The queues enable retailers to sell extra items that the bored customers would normally ignore, by carefully placing them near the till point. Some unscrupulous supermarkets have even adopted drastic measures to slow queues that they have deemed to be moving too fast; such as hiring white haired little old ladies to hold up a queue while they pay for their items with the exact money, in small change, one coin at a time. Furthermore, some supermarkets deliberately use narrow aisles to create a slower flow of customers. One large supermarket chain has recently discussed creating a complex maze out of the aisles to hold customers indefinitely.

'Come on, this way,' directed Death as he pushed his way through the crowds starting to mill around the entrance to the Ponte Vecchio. 'Bloody economists,' he muttered under his breath as he passed a group of Japanese men standing around in dark blue suits taking photos.

Taking the road to the right which ran alongside the Arno river, the companions soon reached the Ponte Santa Trinita successfully leaving the throngs behind them. Death stopped just short of the bridge and turned to face the others.

'And here we are, one of the essential places to visit when in Florence,' he announced in the manner of a tour guide.

The others all peered past Death to look in awe at the bridge, its corners marked with magnificent statue adorned pillars.

'Not the bridge,' tutted Death. 'The ice cream emporium. Come on they do the best ice cream this side of Milan.

'Have we got time to stop for ice cream?' questioned Reg. 'A lot of people are depending on us. I mean aren't we supposed to be saving the world?'

'Wasn't it William Henry Davies that said, what is this life, full of care, if we have no time to stand and eat ice cream?

'I don't think W.H. Davies ever said that,' interjected Bostock.

'Oh. Must have been Mussolini then. I always get those two mixed up. Come on, I'm buying.'

'Well I suppose even if your job is saving the world you should be entitled to a mandatory fifteen minute break for every five hours worked. With that in mind, and only in support of hard earned workers' rights of course, I'll have a rum and raisin,' requested Reg.

'Rum and raisin,' tutted Bostock.

'What's wrong with rum and raisin?'

'For the true ice cream connoisseur, an aficionado of gelatinous flavours, the only flavour of true merit to assess the quality of ice cream is vanilla.'

'Okay so that's one rum and raisin, one vanilla. Eleri?'

'I'll go with vanilla.'

'Oh come on live a little.'

'Well what do you suggest?'

'They do a cherry coke flavour here. Trust me it's worth dying for.'

'Okay.'

Death quickly put the order in, and well within the fifteen minute break perimeter that Reg deemed within their working rights, the party was crossing the Ponte Santa Trinita ice cream cones in hand.

'I must admit this ice cream is really delicious,' conceded Eleri.

'Yes but you're not able to get a true indication of the quality,' said Bostock a slightly jealous look upon his face over the choices made. 'Your flavours are far too overpowering.'

Death had resisted the temptation of adding a sprinkling of chopped nuts to the Professor's cone. He regretted it now.

'I've gotta say comrade, it was impressive the way you ordered the ice cream in Italian,' said Reg in between licking melting ice cream from his fingers.

'That wasn't Italian,' said Death flatly.

'Wasn't it?'

'Nope it was badly spoken Italian. There's a difference.'

'There is?'

'Yep. See what people don't realise is that during the tourist season Florence's population increases twenty times. For every twenty people here only one is an actual resident.'

'Really?'

'Yep. That means that Italian is in fact a minority language. Of course people don't know this so they try and speak Italian while they're visiting. Which is generally a poor attempt. So in fact badly spoken Italian is the majority's spoken language. You learn that sort of thing when you're as widely travelled as me. In my line of work you can turn up anywhere.'

'One other thing. I know you're worldly travelled, but are you sure we're going the right way?' asked Reg. 'I mean the map sort of indicates that the Palazzo dei Cartelloni is that way.' Reg pointed to a road leading off to the left they had just past.

'You can't trust maps Reggie boy,' said Death. 'It wasn't so long ago that cartographers put *Here Be Dragons* if they didn't know an area. And you know what? There weren't any dragons, not one. Those areas usually just contained a couple of natives who generally thought the explorers were simply funnily dressed Gods. Okay so every now and then they'd eat someone but there were no dragons. You just can't trust maps.'

'I think you'll find cartographers have moved on since then,' snorted Bostock.

'Not really. It's just now they put symbols for sites of historical interest on them to keep people away. People are always complaining that the reason they got lost was because their travelling companion doesn't know how to read a map. But maybe they do know how to read a map, it's just the map is wrong. They never think of that do they? You always hear of drivers ending up stuck in rivers because their sat-nav apparently went wrong. Well the sat-nav only goes on the information it's given and that comes from the map. We need to bear left here.'

'That's what the map said,' pointed out Reg.

'Yes, true. But we can't trust following the map. Just because it happens to coincide with the same direction we need to go in.'

'Like if it happens to suggest bearing right shortly down this street,' said Eleri looking over Reg's shoulder at the map.

'Exactly.'

Despite what many may consider to be Death's fanciful tirade against maps, cartographers can be a group of deceitful gits. Two years ago a group of Australian deep sea explorers came across a previously undiscovered island. Although in defence of explorers world-wide it was a relatively small island, only seven miles by nine miles, nevertheless it caused much chagrin amongst the explorer and cartographer international community. An emergency meeting was immediately held in Brussels to discuss this new find. It was quickly realised that its discovery could cause their professions much embarrassment. For years they had been looking to deep oceans and the night sky for new places to explore and then *wallop* someone goes and finds a new island right in their backyard. They would be a laughing stock. Although the island held little in the way of scientific importance (the only unique species was a type of squirrel that fed off the abundant coconuts on the island), they realised that the island would nevertheless almost certainly be world-wide news. In a unanimous vote it was decided that they would keep the discovery a secret until the next batch of maps were due out and they could just sneak it in and hope nobody would notice. At this point a particularly devious cartographer pointed out that naming the island after a religious festival day may aid the subterfuge. After all they always used days of the Church's calendar in olden days when all these islands were originally being discovered. Trouble was all the best ones were already there; Christmas, Easter and Ascension. Even Pentecost had got a look in. After much rummaging and intense cross referencing the small insignificant island deep in the Pacific Ocean was named; Mothering Sunday Island.

The party followed Death as he picked his way through the twists and turns of the Florentine streets, without the aid of the map whatsoever! Although he did regularly check *just to make sure the mapmakers had got it right.* The streets soon changed from the tourist dominated thoroughfares to the day to day working streets of Florence. Dominated by groups of men hanging out on any available corner, standing around chatting in their soiled vest tops, it soon became apparent that they had entered the *not* working streets of Florence. The roads narrowed and became colder as the three to four storey buildings loomed overhead blocking out the sun. Only the tops of the buildings received the illuminating sunlight. Long tall windows were barred and shuttered throughout the high fronted streets. Away from the tourist trail, rough street stalls and graffiti pervaded the narrow roads. It was the sort of place you wouldn't normally frequent unless it was to play the role of victim.

The group subconsciously moved in tighter around Death. It was one of those rare, yet not wholly unique moments when you feel safer being closer to Death.

'Here it is,' announced Death pulling up sharply causing Reg to bump into his back.

'Well it certainly fits the bill,' said Bostock. 'If I

wanted to build a secret headquarters for terrorist scientists this would be it. Far away from the prying eyes of the church and other officials. And look at its construction, the front in a different more dominating style to the two sides, it looks like three smaller buildings.'

Death reluctantly had to agree with Bostock. 'I think we may have found the Galileists headquarters.'

'Apart from one thing of course,' said Eleri who had moved closer to the huge double doors of the building. 'It says on this sign that it's an art school.'

'What?' said Death moving next to Eleri. 'Bugger!'

'It could be a cunning ruse. I'll check what Caesaro has to say about it,' said Bostock pulling out the article the professor had given him. 'Oh.'

'Oh? What do you mean oh?' Death didn't like the word oh. He'd used it enough times to know that it rarely meant anything good.

'Caesaro says here that although he strongly believes that the Palazzo dei Cartelloni was almost certainly once used as the headquarters of the Galileists it is no longer the case and in recent years has been home to the School of Fine Arts.'

'Ah that's what you mean by oh. We've just dragged ourselves all the way over here wasting a lot of time because you haven't done your job properly.'

'What do you mean my job? You didn't read it either.'

'I mean, it's my job to lead, to take us around the place, Reg's job to... er, to er.'

'It's my job to act as protector to my comrades on this mission, being a Vengeance Angel,' declared Reg.

'Yes that's it. And your job to read things.'

'What about Eleri? What's her job?' asked Bostock.

'It's her job to document our mission,' Death turned to Eleri. 'You're not going to write any of this down are you?'

'Well it is my job on this mission,' said Eleri.

'Right yes. Let's just forget about jobs shall we and just move on. No need to be so rigid about what we're supposed to be doing or who's to blame. Er, does the journal say anything else we might need to know?'

'A journal is a type of book isn't it?' interrupted Reg. 'Remember when Jenny's bible hit the Demon Bacchaus in the head? Well now I know what it means to throw the book at someone. Ha ha.'

'You've been waiting a long time to say that haven't you?' asked Death.

'Well yes, but book comments don't come up that often,' replied Reg in his own defence.

'I don't really think *come up* is the right phrase, I think *prised in* is more suitable.'

'Well it is a funny line though isn't it.'

'At the time maybe, but there is a sort of time limit on that sort of thing. About a minute after the event. At tops three minutes and only if it is an extremely funny and witty line.'

'It is an extremely witty line.'

'That is debatable. But I think, and I don't believe I'd be alone in this, that eight months later can't really be considered a quick witty response.'

'Really?' said a crestfallen Reg. 'Well I did have a lot on my mind at the time.'

'Caesaro says that the facade on the front of the building was to mark the building as the headquarters of the Galileists. As well as the bust of Galileo, two large cartouches list his great discoveries,' said Bostock bringing the others back to the job in hand.

The others all looked up to the large bas-relief panels, shaped in the form of two gigantic scrolls placed either side of Galileo's bust on the building's exterior.

'Well maybe there's a clue in the lists of his works,'

suggested Eleri. 'I'll take the one on the left you take the one on the right.'

Death duly moved to the right, with Reg closely in tow, however despite his best efforts, namely standing on tip toes, Reg couldn't get a good enough angle to read the inscriptions.

'These streets are too narrow to read the writing,' he complained.

'Don't worry you're not missing much,' replied Eleri from the other side. 'The writing on my panel is too worn to properly make out. How about yours?'

'Doesn't seem to be much in the way of clues,' responded Death. 'But I can make out a few things. It eludes to Galileo's work. His observations of the planet Jupiter and using the telescope to work out longitudes at sea. Wait what's this?'

The others looked eagerly across at Death.

'Geometry. He also did Geometry.'

'So that's who's to blame for all those tedious school lessons,' muttered Eleri.

Death looked at his pocket watch. 'I think we're wasting valuable time here. It's pretty obvious that the Galileists have long since moved on. We'd better check out that other place.'

'Anton Gabbiani's fresco at the Pitti Palace,' stated Bostock.

'That's the one. Bound to be a clue there.'

'Why the sudden confidence?' asked Eleri. 'This one has obviously been a dead end.'

'It's our last possible chance of finding the Galileist headquarters. And that's how this sort of thing always works. It's always on your last chance you get lucky.'

Chapter 18

Every city has numerous municipal gardens and parks, presenting a somewhat idealised view of the city for both tourists and residents alike. Like some second rate magician distracting the eye from the card hidden up his sleeve, their purpose is to draw attention away from the uglier areas within the city borders. They represent an archetypical view of nature, with their neatly trimmed hedgerows and flowerbeds scattered beside meandering paths and tinkling waterways (and yet they scream out that this is what the whole city could have looked like if tons of concrete hadn't been poured on top of it).

Even the beautiful city of Florence has such gardens to draw attention away from the grime ridden streets within its bowels. The most famous of these is the Boboli Gardens and overlooking them stands one of the grandest of buildings in the city of Florence, the former residence of the Medici family; the Pitti Palace.

'Well it just looks like a typical example of the ruling class' ostentatiousness if you ask me,' commented Reg as they entered the palace. 'I mean you don't get a house like this without someone suffering for it.'

'The Medici family were great patrons of the arts and sciences,' responded the Professor. 'Without them we wouldn't have many of the great examples of high art we have today.'

'Well I'm just saying that it's built on the sweat and toil of the honest workers.'

'Will you two stop bickering,' snapped Death. 'This is our last chance to find the Galileist's headquarters and I need everyone concentrating on the job in hand. I for one don't fancy explaining to Archangel Michael that we failed because we couldn't decide whether the Medici's were great patrons of the arts and sciences for the betterment of mankind or just a bunch of showoff tyrants.'

'Showoff tyrants,' whispered Reg to Bostock before declaring aloud. 'Right you are comrade, more important things at hand.'

Reg quickly took a few strides away from Bostock leaving the blustering Professor behind.

'Look at this,' said Eleri drawing the others attention to a large painting in front of her.

'Is it a clue?' asked Reg as he joined her.

'No it's a picture of Death. I didn't realise you were *that* famous,' she said giggling.

'Oh yeah laugh it up. They never get it right,' grumbled Death.

'Ah yes very reminiscent of Breugel in its approach,' commented the Professor examining the skeletal figure at the centre of the painting.

'Indeed. The artist has really captured your likeness,' added Eleri imitating the Professor.

'It's nothing like me and well you know it. They always do this. Oh we need a portrayal of Death, I know, a skeleton carrying a scythe, that will do,' ranted Death. 'I mean do I look like a skeleton to you? At most I'd say I was slim, most would probably describe me as athletic.'

'Well you have got a slightly bony quality,' observed Eleri looking Death up and down.

'I have a strong bone structure that's all, I inherited it from my mother. Come on we need to find this Sala Meridiana place,' said Death walking off muttering to himself. 'Most people complain about their passport photos, look what I have to deal with.'

'According to Caesaro, the Sala Meridiana is just up ahead in the south west corner of the palace,' said

Bostock catching up with Death. 'Next to the *Mueso del Costume.*'

The party made their way to the Sala Meridiana with Eleri and Reg walking slightly behind still giggling at Death's reaction to the painting. Death and Bostock suddenly stopped just short of the entrance.

'Oh dear,' said Bostock turning to face Eleri and Reg. 'The entrance is cordoned off and there's a rather official looking guard.'

'Are you quite sure that's the entrance to the Sala Meridiana?' asked Reg.

'Caesaro does mention that it's rarely visited,' said Bostock referring to the journal.

'Well now we know why,' responded Reg.

'Maybe I could distract him,' suggested Eleri undoing the top button of her top and flicking her hair. 'You know with my womanly charms.'

Death gave Eleri an appraising look. 'Er, perhaps not this time. We'll use the age old Italian tradition.'

'And what's that?' asked a slightly disgruntled Eleri.

'Bribery.'

The word bribery is believed to have first entered the English language in the fourteenth century. Although the origin of the word is unknown, as it was decided that it was best to keep that sort of thing quiet. It is however, almost universally accepted that the practise of bribery had gone on long before that. Most probably brought over with the Romans along with their roads and aqueducts. The case for this is quite strong as planning permission is extremely difficult to obtain without some act of bribery occurring. Luckily for Death and the others, the guard standing in front of the entrance represented a low level Italian official. Not that it made him any more susceptible to bribery than other Italian officials, it just made him a whole lot cheaper.

The guard moved from his slovenly position leaning

against the wall and stood to what he regarded as attention. After a brief conversation and the exchange of a couple of neatly folded pieces of paper, the guard went for a rest break. Death nodded to the others to follow him as he stepped over the red cord rope that marked the boundary to the Sala Meridiana; the room that contained Gabbiani's famous fresco and the last known clue to the ancient residence of the Galileists.

In a jaw-dropping cliché, all four stood mouths gaping open in silence for a moment, as they looked up at the ceiling fresco's vivid colours and workmanship. Reg was the first to speak.

'Well comrades I must admit that this display of opulence, albeit at the expense of the working masses, is magnificent.'

'Yes,' agreed Bostock. 'It truly is Gabbiani's finest work.'

'So is Galileo the beardy fella in the centre?' asked Reg.

'No that figure is Chronos.'

'Who?'

'Father Time.'

'How do you know that?'

'It's to do with the cleverly crafted symbology of the piece,' explained the Professor. 'See the neighbouring putti, the chereb like figures surrounding Father Time? If you look they are holding a scythe, circle and hourglass, the symbols of Father Time.'

'I thought they were your symbols,' said Reg turning towards Death.

'Yes they are. That's where we get them from. Time catches up with everyone, eventually. Time and Death sort of go hand in hand. Father Time was the founder of the whole Death Organisation, retired now of course. We kind of dropped the circle thing though.'

'Does he really look like that?'

'Never met the old guy. He's a bit of a recluse these days. Left the department long before I joined.'

Reg turned back to Bostock.

'So which one's Galileo?'

'The other beardy figure, over on the side. Behind the cannon.'

'Oh. What's that other thing next to him?'

'It's called an armillary sphere. It's used for fixing the positions of planets.'

'Full of questions aren't you Reg,' commented Death.

'Well if we're going solve this thing I think it'd be better if we're all on the same page. Comrades together.'

'I don't often get to say this Reg, but you're right. Bostock fill us in. You know all about this symbology stuff.'

'Well yes, lucky to have me here really. I do know quite a lot about this sort of thing. Father Time I've explained. The woman on his arm is Knowledge or Scienza.'

'Science.'

'Yes Reg science,' replied Bostock. 'The figure under his foot with the donkey's ears is Ignorance. Galileo's pupil described the work as *Time raising up Arts and Sciences to the temple of glory and trampling Ignorance.*'

'Catchy title,' said Death.

'Yes indeed. But I guess it does tell us what's going on. Especially if you think of the timing of the work. Ignorance is regarded as the Church's Inquisition. It's basically saying that it's just a matter of time before science will win over the Church.'

'That's pretty heretical stuff,' said Death taking a step back to get a better view of the whole scene. 'I think we might just be on the right track. This is definitely the sort of thing the Galileists would use as a marker. What about the other stuff? That woman holding a clock?'

'I believe she is just a further representation of the time theme. The cannon in front of Galileo...'

'It represents a castle or fort right,' interrupted Reg.

'To the uneducated mind perhaps,' said Bostock. 'It symbolises Galileo's work on ballistics. Likewise, the armillary sphere denotes his work on the cosmos and planets.'

'Eleri read out that clue the er, *Solaris Linearis,*' asked Death.

'Those who seek enlightened truth. Beneath Medici's stars. Solarus does the line provide. And time does show the path.'

'Okay. Right. Those who seek enlightened truth. The Galileists. Agreed?' Death turned to the others who nodded their agreement. 'Beneath Medici's stars; Florence. That leaves us with; Solarus does the line provide. And time does show the path. Anything?'

'Father Time is pointing towards Galileo. Maybe that could indicate some sort of direction. Time does show the path,' suggested Bostock. 'But there isn't any line of the sun.'

'That armillo sphere thing. Wouldn't that have the sun on it?'

Death, Bostock and Reg all moved a bit closer to the armillary sphere to get a better look.

'I can't see anything that could be a line,' said Reg.

'Neither can I,' responded Death. 'And I'm a lot closer to the ceiling than you.'

'What's that grey splotch behind Galileo?' asked Reg. 'I can't really make it out, but it looks like a castle.'

'Reg, what is your obsession with castles?' asked Bostock. 'It is most likely a tower, to represent his experiments at the Leaning Tower of Pisa, on free fall and mass. I think we need to look at this from another angle. What if we think of Galileo himself as the sun? A sort of guiding light, a beacon so to speak.'

'Does that help?' asked Death.

'Not at the moment but give me a second.'

'Professor. What's this?'

The others turned to Eleri who was on her hands and knees examining a metal strip that ran along the floor and up the wall.

'That's the Meridian Line. It's how this room got it's name; the Sala Meridiana. It's the former apartment of Ferdinando de' Medici son of Grand Duke Cosimo III.'

Death and Reg both exchanged glances whilst Eleri raised her eyebrows at Bostock.

'Yes, there used to be a hole in the fresco so light could shine through. At noon the light would shine on the Meridian Line corresponding with the date marked on the line.'

'Really?' asked Eleri.

'Yes. You can still see where the hole was. See near the base of that tree?' The Professor turned to face the fresco again.

'No, I mean really?'

'What?' asked the Professor turning back from the fresco, slightly annoyed at the interruption. He was quite sure he was on to something here.

'There's a metal strip that uses the sun in this room.'

'Oh.'

'He's finally got there,' announced Death. 'We've been looking in the wrong place. The line of the sun is on the floor. Not on the fresco at all!'

Damn it, thought Professor Bostock. How could he have been so slow picking up on that clue? If this got out he'd be the laughing stock of the Angelic Times' Crossword Puzzlers' Society. Although in his defence it was more of a physical puzzle than one based on words alone. It didn't help.

'That other line,' said Reg. 'Beneath Medici's stars. Not just Florence but this room. It was owned by a

Medici son of Cosimo as in Cosmos maybe, as in stars. And beneath, on the floor not on the ceiling.'

'Yer, I think we've all got there now Reg,' said Death patting him on the shoulder. 'Okay so we're agreed this is obviously the Solarus line. Now we need time to show the path. Professor you said the sun shone on the line at noon, right?'

'Yes at noon,' confirmed the Professor breaking from his own self admonishment. 'The Meridian Line runs from the two solstices giving the date of each day inbetween.'

'Can anyone think how noon would show the path?' asked Death. 'It's midday, 12'o'clock.'

'It's lunch time,' added Reg.

'That would still only give us one point on the line. And that's today's date which we already know,' pointed out the Professor. 'It must be a separate line. It's got to be in the fresco somewhere. Father Time is pointing to Galileo. It's got to be here.'

'And time does show the path,' said Eleri repeating the mystery line aloud.

'Time, time, something with time,' muttered Death, studying the fresco. 'Come on people we need the time.'

'Then look at your watch, ha ha,' joked Reg.

Eleri and Death looked at each other sharply, then up at the fresco.

'The clock!' they announced in unison.

'The figure holding the clock,' continued Death. 'It's nine twenty-two on the clock! If we take the line of the sun through the hole at nine twenty-two it'll give us a different line.'

'I don't understand this comrades. How does it work?' asked Reg. 'I mean it'll give us a second point in this room, but the Galileists are obviously not here.'

Bostock and Death looked dumbfounded by Reg's question.

'Well it's a start. At least we're getting somewhere,' replied Death.

'It's Geometry!' declared Eleri. 'It's bloody geometry.'

'What?' said Death turning to her.

'We've got two points and their angles. You can work out a third point where their lines intersect,' explained Eleri. 'It's basic geometry. Remember the facade? Galileo was famous for his work in geometry.'

'Okay people, lets go to work,' said Death clapping his hands together. 'I'll find that security guard and see if I can bribe us some more time. Eleri take my phone and see if you can find out where the sun was at nine twenty-two. There's bound to be an app somewhere that'll tell us that sort of thing. Reg take this money and go buy some string, a ruler and a protractor.'

'What shall I do?' asked Bostock.

Death gave the Professor an appraising look up and down.

'Go next door to the *Museo del Costume*.'

'Yes?'

'And see if you can get any fashion tips.'

Question: How do you buy a protractor, a ruler and a piece of string in Italy?

Answer: You use the phrase: *Posso acquistare un goniometro, un righello e un pezzo di spago*?

Question: How do you buy a protractor, a ruler and a piece of string in Italy when you don't speak Italian?

Answer: See below.

Reg looked down the shop lined street. The most likely candidate to stock the items he needed was a large shop almost three quarters of the way down. In the English speaking world it could be described as a convenience store, but this was Italy and when you don't speak Italian convenient is not a word that springs to mind. He entered the store to be greeted by a large array of items, none of which appeared to hold any logical order or placement. After a short while wandering aimlessly around, Reg decided help was most certainly required and approached the counter.

'Do you speak English?' Reg asked the middle-aged man behind the counter.

'Nossignore.'

'Ah, er...'

The shop assistant stroked his designer stubbled chin. 'Si parla Francese?'

'Erm no.'

'Si parla Tedesco, er German?'

'No.'

'Parla Cinese?'

'Erm. Oh Chinese.'

'Si Chinese.'

'Ah no.'

'Si parla Russo, Russian? Parla Olandese, Dutch? Parla Arabo, erm Arabic?'

'No, no and no.' replied Reg with his best Italian accent. How could someone know all these languages and not English.

'Ah,' the shop assistant raised a finger triumphantly. 'Si parla Finlandese?'

Reg sunk his head onto the counter. 'No,' he mumbled. Now this was ridiculous. Nobody speaks Finnish; even people from Finland try to avoid using it as much as possible. Why hadn't he ever learnt any languages? The only Italian he really knew was based around the food you found in supermarkets. What good is lasagne now? Spaghetti! Someone had once told him spaghetti was Italian for string!

'Spaghetti. I want spaghetti!' declared Reg raising his head triumphantly.

'Ah si, spaghetti,' responded the assistant smiling. 'Pasta.'

The smiling assistant pointed to a shelf on the right with multiple packets of pasta.

'No spaghetti.'

'Si. pasta.'

'No. Spaghetti.'

'Si. Pasta,' responded the assistant pointing at the pasta shelf.

'No. Not pasta. Spa-ghett-i,' said Reg trying the age old method of communication between languages by speaking very slowly and pronounced.

'Pasta.'

What is more remarkable than believing that the speak slowly, more pronounced, and if possible a bit more loudly, approach will actually work, is the fact that despite its failure, people after a short pause will try it again.

'Spa-ghett-i.'

'Si. Pasta!'

It was time for a different approach. With a subtle universal hand movement Reg indicated he wanted a pen and paper. The assistant duly responded. After a brief moments contemplation Reg realised the flaw with this approach. How do you draw string? It was basically a line. He tried it anyway.

'Pasta?' asked the assistant hopefully.

The hand gesture had worked pretty well though. Maybe he could try and mime string. Holding an imaginary piece of string between his fingers, he began to tie an equally imaginary bow.

'Spago?' asked the assistant tentatively.

'Spago... String?'

The assistant pointed to several balls of string neatly stacked on the counter less than a foot away from Reg. Granted not as impressive as the offering in Cawker

City, Kansas, or even Little Merit for that matter, but still string.

'String! Spago! Spago!' shouted Reg gleefully.

Okay now for a protractor.

Sometimes it's easier in life just to learn the phrase... *Posso acquistare un goniometro, un righello e un pezzo di spago*?

Unsurprisingly Reg was the last to return to the Sala Meridiana.

'Here you go. One protractor, one ruler and a ball of string,' announced Reg presenting the items to Death.

'Well done.'

'Where did that come from?' asked Reg, indicating a large ladder propped against the wall under the fresco.

'I procured it on my travels,' said Death.

'You mean you stole it!'

'Borrowed. The word is borrowed.'

'Sorry comrade but I must say I disapprove. Some hard working workman, a window cleaner or the like, is without the tools of his trade.'

'Relax Reg I left a note. Anyway I think I've already spent enough. That guard demanded double the going rate for a bribe of this nature. That's the trouble with Florence everything is so expensive, even the bribes. And you know, I can't even claim it back on expenses. The Heavenly realm tends to frown on that sort of transaction.'

'Well if you did leave a note, then I suppose the ends justify the means.'

'Yer and I'm pretty sure he'll find a way off the balcony sooner or later.'

'What you left him stuck halfway up a building?'

'Relax Reg he'll find a way down. Right now we need to concentrate on what we are doing here. I need you to climb to the top of the ladder.'

'Why me?' asked Reg looking up at the vast length of the ladder stretching up before him. 'I mean I'm the shortest. I'll never reach that hole in the fresco.'

'You don't have to reach, I'm going to be standing on your shoulders.'

'What? Why are you standing on my shoulders?'

Death gave a sigh.

'Because it's the only way we'll reach the fresco. And lets face it we're hardly going to do it the other way around. I'm not having those platformed shoes of yours on my shoulders. This suit is a Vespucci you know.'

'For your information my shoes are not platformed. They've just got thick soles. And that's not what I'm talking about. It's not about whose standing on whose shoulders, it's about the risk factor. As a former union representative I must point out that this seriously contravenes health and safety guidelines. Someone could get seriously hurt.' And that someone is probably going to be me, thought Reg. Death had a way of getting out of all kinds of scrapes.

'Okay. Okay. Eleri pass me my phone.' Death quickly hit the speed dial button. 'Hey Negligence. Death 221 here. How's it going buddy? I was just wondering, have you got any work on inside the Pitti Palace today? Any accidents anything like that?'

'I'll just check. Nah. Oh wait. Some fella is about to fall off a balcony any second now. Just outside. Breaks his leg that's all.'

Ah hah. I knew he'd find a way down,' said Death looking pointedly at Reg. 'Any other incidents?'

'Other than that nothing.'

'Cheers mate,' said Death hanging up the phone. 'Okay you happy now? Negligence is one of the Four Horsemen of Everyday Life; his department deals with all the accidents and he says we're in the clear. So get climbing Reggie boy!'

Grumbling to himself Reg began his climb to the top of the ladder.

'Eleri take this end of the string,' said Death before joining Reg on his ascent.

At the top Death clambered precariously over Reg's back and onto his shoulders.

'Are you sure this is safe?' Grunted Reg through clenched teeth as he bore the full weight of Death on his shoulders.

'You heard, I checked with Negligence. He deals with all accidents, as well as deaths. It's to make sure nobody exceeds their allotted amount of near death lucky escapes. He covers all mortals. Oh wait. You're not mortal are you? You're a solid incarnation of a soul and I'm well, I'm Death. Oh well.'

'Oh that's just great! And just for the record comrade; before I plunge to my death or my banishment or whatever it is. I'm a trainee Vengeance Angel not an incarnation of a soul.'

Ignoring Reg's complaint, Death held the string up against the blocked hole in the fresco.

'Right. Eleri pull up the slack on the string.'

'Wait a sec,' shouted Eleri checking her phone. 'The sun was slightly more to the left.'

'Hurry up!' Reg's face had taken on a shade of purple and sweat was starting to bead at his temple.

'Okay here,' said Eleri holding her end of the string to the wall.

Death held his section of string to the fresco with his thumb and dropped the remaining ball to the floor.

'Okay Professor, take the other end and line it up with today's date on the *Sala Meridiana.*'

Bostock quickly followed Death's instructions, then paused.

'Erm. Does anybody know what the date is today? Is it the 23rd or 24th?'

'It's the 24th!' yelled Reg. His legs had begun to twitch under the strain and when he thought of them the word *spago* strang to mind.

'Oh dear,' said Bostock despondently and lowered shoulders. 'That's a pity.'

'What's a pity?' asked Eleri, concern crossing her face.

'Well it's the third Wednesday of the month.'

'And?'

'It's Kazam's day to compile the Angelic Times' crossword. He does it every first and third Wednesday of the month. He's my favourite. Quite a trickster he is. He did this quite frankly brilliant play on words concerning cheese a few months back. Of course Kazam isn't his real name, nobody knows who he is. Might even be a woman. But all of us in the Angelic Times crossword puzzlers society think he's a man. He has to use the pseudonym to prevent being inundated with fan mail and the problem of stalkers.'

'I think saving the world might just take precedence over Kazam's crossword,' shouted down Death. 'And I don't think Reg's legs can take much more.'

'Yes I suppose saving the world is more important,' replied Bostock as he quickly bent down to place the other end of the string to the corresponding date on the sala meridiania. 'Besides if we hurry I might be able to pick up a late edition.'

Death pulled out the protractor from his inside pocket and measured the angle the three points now gave them.

'It's about 89.9 degrees.'

'About. We need this to be accurate,' insisted Eleri from below.

'Eleri, I'm standing on the shoulders of a short man on top of a very wobbly ladder. I don't think accuracy is an option here.'

'Can we perhaps hurry up here comrades?'

Death twisted his position slightly and threw the protractor down to Bostock who quickly measured the angle at his end.

'Okay got it,' confirmed Bostock as soon as he'd finished.

'Now mark the string so I can measure the length,' instructed Eleri. 'We'll need the distance between the two angles to work out the final point.

Death marked the point on the string that had been pressed against the fresco with his thumbnail and began his decent. Reg gave an audible sign of relief as Death got off his back.

Reaching the bottom Death passed Eleri the string.

'Okay off you go Eleri. Do the sums.'

'Can't you do it? I'm a little rusty with my geometry.'

'The only measurements that interested me during maths lessons were Tricia Hardy's. And the only equation I ever studied was how I could make a; her, plus b; me, equal c; fun times. Never did work that one out though. Mainly due to the variable d; Justin Locke, her boyfriend. So as you can imagine I don't really understand all that Menelaus' triangle stuff.

'I think you mean Pythagoras' triangle,' interrupted Bostock. 'Menelaus was an ancient greek king. Pythgoras was the mathematician.

'Well volunteered,' said Eleri passing Bostock the string.

'Yes well done Professor,' Death said, congratulating Bostock with a few sarcastically delivered slaps on the shoulder.

'Well I suppose I am the most qualified to work it out.'

'Oh and for the record, Menelaus was involved in a triangle,' said Death smiling. 'A love triangle to be precise. Between him, Paris and Helen of Troy. A lot like me, Tricia and Justin. Although his involved more killing and less mathematics.

'Maybe we could get lunch while the Professor here, works out the sums,' suggested Eleri.

'It won't take that long. It is a simple equation,' Bostock paused and looked at his fellow companions before adding. 'For me.'

'Well we could grab a quick panini,' said Eleri taking out her note pad. 'What does everyone want? There's a stall just outside.'

'Something with goat's cheese,' requested Bostock his head now deeply submerged in his calculations.

'I'll have extra finely sliced prosciutto, roasted red peppers, not green, red. Fresh mozzarella, and chopped basil,' said Death. 'Oh, and if they try to offer olive tapenade threaten them with violence. Olives have their place in paninis and that's as oil and nothing else. Have you got all that?'

'Yes, I do shorthand.'

'Are you sure?' asked Death.

'Yes of course,' replied Eleri turning her notepad towards Death.

'It says ham and cheese.'

'Yes. Like I said, I write shorthand.' Eleri turned her notepad towards Reg.

'I've never had a panini before.'

'Really?'

'Yes really. I don't believe in all this posh food,' grumbled Reg. 'All these swanky cafe bars, with their middle class food, have caused the demise of the good old cafes, where a cup of coffee didn't cost you a good proportion of your hard earned wage.

Reg did in fact have a very strict dietary regime. Although it had nothing to do with his ever expanding waistline. It had to do with his political ideology. Anything *a la carte* stayed off his menu. When he visited restaurants, (and he did occasionally eat out, but only as part of a celebratory event, any other occasion would be far too bourgeois) he always chose what he considered to be the most working class meal available. Reg liked his potatoes boiled, roasted, or chipped, certainly not sautéed or au gratin, and his mashed potatoes were never piped. Reg ate meals that sounded proletarian; ploughman's lunch, steak and ale pie (the combination of ale and pie aided its earthy appeal).

In fact the word pie usually helped his decision, shepherd's pie, fisherman's pie; the working class professions had pies, the bourgeoisie didn't have pies. The bourgeoisie ate food with fancy French titles like coq au vin and beef bourguignon. In the past Reg's politically based cuisine had worked in his favour; the best meal he'd ever had was in a typically middle class restaurant. He'd complained that he didn't want any bourgeois au poivre sauce with his steak and the chef had made him a peppercorn sauce instead. He'd even boiled then fried the potatoes instead of giving him the sautéed ones.

'Okay so you don't want anything,' said Eleri closing her note pad.

Reg's gurgling stomach told him otherwise; it wasn't so interested in the political ramifications of panini.

'Er, actually. I suppose we are in Italy and in Italy a panini is just a sandwich. So I guess I should share the food of my Italian working class comrades, I'll have the same as Death.

'Cancel the food order. I worked out the result,' declared the Professor.

'Oh great, nice one Reg. If you hadn't dithered we'd have a plethora of panini on the way,' said Death.

Eleri looked up from her notepad. 'A plethora of panini?'

'That's the correct collective term for a group of

sandwiches, and panini are apparently just Italian sandwiches. You know, just like a murder of crows, a parliament of owls, a superfluity of nuns,' explained Death. 'A plethora of sandwiches.'

'Plethora just means a lot of something. It is not a collective term.'

'Exactly it means a lot of sandwiches.'

'I don't think food has collective terms. Well not in its cooked form anyway.'

'Course it does. There's a cornucopia of pasties, a botulism of kebabs, and a suspicion of omelettes.'

'You're just making them up!'

'They all sound like they're just made up. Look at a flange of baboons, that just sounds like it has been made up for comedy purposes. There's a pleasure of ice-cream, a cholesterol of hamburgers, a bingo of boiled ham and parsley sauce.'

'Made up, made up, made up.'

'There's a nubble of ...'

'Sorry to interrupt your debate comrades,' said Reg, drawing their attention with a raised hand. 'But why is it my fault? You took longer than me to decide what panini to have.'

'You had all the time I spent deciding to make up your mind too. It's called planning ahead Reg,' said Death. 'I did not get to be head of my department without definitive forward planning.'

'Er. I've done the calculations,' said Bostock. 'What do you want to do with them?'

'Not sure. I guess we'll just see where it points and go from there.'

'I've got a map!' Reg pulled out the folded map and laid it out on the floor.

'From my calculations the Galileist Headquarters would appear to be somewhere in this mountainous region here,' said Bostock, pointing to a section of the map outside Florence. 'Although of course there is a slight margin for error, but I think we should start by concentrating our efforts in this zone.'

Eleri leant over the map pushing her hair out of her eyes. 'There are two villages in that area. What are we supposed to do, knock on every door and ask if the Galileists live here?'

'Well it's a plan,' said Death. 'Not a very good one, but it is a plan.'

'Yes. But we are on a timescale here remember?' responded Eleri. 'We just haven't got the time to go around door to door. Although, maybe we could ask if they've seen any scientists around?'

'What like asking directions? They are a secret organisation. The key word being secret. Excuse me have you seen anyone wandering around in a white coat wearing protective goggles? They might have a bunsen burner in their back pocket.'

'Well they might know. Oh wait I forgot you're men, you don't ask for directions.'

'I still feel we are missing something,' said Bostock pacing in a circle around the map. 'Another clue or similar. Yes our co-ordinates are approximate but so were the maps of 1693. 1693!'

Bostock looked at the others as if he expected them to jump up and hug him.

'Yes 1693 the year that the fresco was painted,' said a nonplussed Death.

'Exactly! The fresco was painted in 1693. We're looking at a modern map. We should be looking for a structure that was present in 1693. What with the population growth and everything, there would be far fewer buildings back then. What we need to look for is an old building predating 1693. Something like a... oh.'

'Oh?'

Death followed Bostock's gaze up to the fresco and

to the depiction of Galileo standing behind a cannon.

'Something like a castle or fort,' mumbled Bostock.

'So what you're saying is the Galileists' headquarters is in a castle,' said Reg pulling his trousers up at the waist band. 'Like I said.'

'Well yes indeed.'

'It's here!' Interrupted Eleri pointing at the map. 'We've found them. Look an old castle right in the middle of the zone. It's the only one, it must be them!'

The others gathered around the map.

'That's got to be it,' confirmed Death. 'Right let's make a jump and get the plague back.'

'I just need to make a quick phone call,' said Bostock walking to one side.

The others gave him a quizzical look.

'I need to call Caesaro.'

'Why?' Eleri asked with a puzzled expression on her face.

'I'm an academic. It's what we do.'

'What is it that you do?'

'We gloat!' The Professor turned his back and spoke into his phone. 'Ah Caesaro old chap. You know how you've been studying those Galileists for the last twenty years?'

'Yes.'

'Well just thought you'd like to know. I've solved the mystery of the markers. I had a quick look at it this morning. And thought perhaps you might like to know where their ancient headquarters is situated.'

'Oh my dear boy, I presume you're referring to the old castle a few miles outside Florence.'

'Yes. Wait how did you know that?'

'This isn't the seventeenth century now. Scientists don't have to go sneaking around anymore, the Church stopped persecuting them years ago. The modern Galileists are in the phonebook. I even went to one of their charity gala nights a

few years back.'

'And you didn't think to mention this?'

'Well you never asked. I presumed you were interested in the markers not the Galileists themselves. Purely from an academic standpoint you understand. But well done on solving the secret path, my nine year old granddaughter took twice as long to solve it, last year.'

Bostock hung up the phone and returned to the others.

'Well what did he say?' asked Eleri.

'He er, said. Well done. Right we'd better make that jump and get the plague back.'

Chapter 19

Death and the others appeared on a dusty road next to the old stone wall that surrounded the perimeter of the castle. The road followed the wall for a short section before turning towards a set of wrought iron gates.

'Well this is the place,' announced Bostock. 'The ancient headquarters of the Galileists.'

'Are you sure? I mean it doesn't look very scientific.' Reg's idea of science revolved more around solar panels and lasers, than crumbling stonework and dusty roads.

'Oh I'm sure,' mumbled Bostock.

'How can you be sure?'

'Call it an academic hunch.'

The Professor had experienced many academic hunches during his career, granted none had been so fact based that another academic had confirmed it was a fact. Nevertheless, he felt that this hunch was right.

'So what's the plan?' Eleri turned to Death.

'We knock on the door and ask for the plague back,' replied Death confidently.

'Sounds risky comrade. It'll mean they'll know who we are,' said Reg. 'Shouldn't we try subterfuge?'

'Relax Reggie boy. These guys are scientists not ninja warriors. They are hardly going to spring out on us with nunchucks.'

'But what if they refuse?'

'Then we turn to plan B.'

'Oh okay,' replied Reg.

'What's plan B?' Eleri asked.

'Think of a new plan,' said Death over his shoulder, as he strode towards the front gate, brushing dust from his trousers as he went.

'Now this is more like it,' said Reg looking at the entrance to the castle. 'Much more scientific.'

The old wrought iron gates were bedecked with two closed circuit cameras, a keypad locking system, and a state of the art video intercom system.

'That's odd,' said Eleri standing in front of the gates.

'What is?' Death asked.

'All this hi-tech security and the gate is open!' Eleri pushed the gates open wide to emphasise her point.

'Oh good,' said Death walking through the entrance.

'But it isn't normal.'

'Hard to tell really,' replied Death as he walked up the path towards the castle. 'See nothing in my life is what you might call normal, so working out what's odd or not is next to impossible. In fact, it's so close to impossible they may as well be standing next to each other on a tube-train, on the London underground, at 5.34pm on a wet Tuesday evening.'

'You do realise that you're probably insane?

'Really? Why is that?'

'Not being able to tell the difference between what is normal or not is a sign of insanity?'

'Yes, but what is normal?' Death said putting a slightly profound lilt on his voice.

'Exactly the point I'm making.'

'Okay but what about you? Do you think walking up to the front door of a group of terrorist scientists and asking them to return the plague they stole, is the action of a sane person?'

'It was your plan!'

'Yes but it's up to the rest of you to find the flaws in the plan. I'm the one that came up with the plan, you should have found its faults. You can't expect me to do everything.'

'I did find faults with it!'

'And you're still here? Sounds a little bit crazy to me.'

'The door is open too!' said Reg interrupting Death and Eleri's banter.

The huge iron studded oak doors to the castle stood wide open. The group stopped just short of the three large stone steps that led to the doorway.

'I don't like this. I don't like this at all,' said Death 'You should never trust an open door. An open door has no purpose. If you leave a door open you may as well just have a hole in the wall. It's as bad as a locked door. If a door is locked you can't get in. You may as well just carry on with the wall rather than put a hole in it then fill it with a locked door.'

'That's what I have been trying to tell you, albeit without the dubious logic. Something is most definitely wrong,' whispered Eleri.

'Someone may have just left it open by mistake. You know when they were bringing the shopping in or something,' suggested Reg. 'Besides it's just an open door. Doors are supposed to open and close.'

'Right. Well seeing as you appear to be the expert on doors why don't you go first?'

'Well I wouldn't say I'm an expert on the subject, comrade,' said Reg responding to Death's suggestion. 'It's more just a working knowledge.'

'Eleri take a quote,' said Death. 'Mankind is under threat of annihilation and we are all that stand in the way of this. If our lives must be forfeit to this end, then so be it. For it is our responsibility, nay our duty, to complete this task, whatever personal risk that may entail. End quote. Right Reg, off you go.'

'What? Why am I going first?'

'A: I'm not crazy. And B: You're a Vengeance Angel, it's your job to do the risky stuff. Go on we're right behind you, well at an approximate distance, but still fairly close and most definitely behind.'

Reg gave a sigh and moved forward. There was no point in arguing with Death. Reg approached the door, silently cursing his choice of work experience as a Vengeance Angel as he went. With a tentative knock and a *hello* Reg cautiously entered the castle. It seemed appropriate to knock and say hello. People rarely have the confidence to cross another person's boundary without a knock and hello. It is the done thing, even if the door is open. It is also the done thing in horror movies; where the tentative knock and hello is usually followed by a grizzly end. Reg tried to put that thought to the back of his mind as he stepped inside.

It wasn't at all what Reg had expected and he rose from his slightly crouched stance to stand up straight. Several gothic arched doorways at the far end of the long hallway were the only concession to the castle's original style, otherwise the interior was reminiscent of a large corporate firm's foyer. The floor was covered with shiny black tiles, and potted plants were scattered around the area in such a precise way as to make them look randomly placed. The clean white walls were adorned with silver framed photographs of famous scientists. At least Reg presumed they were portraits of famous scientists. He didn't really know that many famous scientists, well not to recognise in a photo anyway. The only one he really knew was Albert Einstein, and that was only because he had once mistakenly identified a photo of him, which turned out to be that of Salvador Dali, during a picture round at the local pub's quiz. They didn't appear to have a picture of Albert Einstein, or Salvador Dali for that matter. Notwithstanding Reg was sure they were pictures of famous scientists. They certainly looked like photos of famous scientists; they were black and white, and very grainy. They were in the most part either wearing white coats or tweedy type suits with bow ties. Some of them were even holding test tubes and petri dishes and the like. They were definitely pictures of famous scientists.

Death's voice broke Reg's study of the pictures.

'Reg?'

'It seems to be all clear. You can come in,' said Reg in a muted shout.

The others entered with a similar crouched stance that Reg had adopted, then straightened up when they saw the interior.

'I think this must be the place,' announced Reg. 'There are pictures of famous scientists on the wall.'

'Oh yes indeed, there's Wilhelm Conrad Roentgen,' said Bostock commenting on the photograph nearest him. 'And Max Planck. I love his work on black-body radiation. Oh and they've put Planck next to Ludwig Boltzmann! Someone's got a sense of humour, wouldn't you say Reg?' Bostock continued, whilst chuckling and giving Reg a nudge.

'Er. They don't appear to have a picture of Albert Einstein,' replied Reg.

'Ha yes. He's reserved for the walls of student digs.'

'Okay enough with spot the famous scientist,' said Death. 'We've got a plague to find. End of mankind and all that, remember?'

'Yes quite,' said Bostock, straightening the lapels on his jacket. 'So which door?'

'Easy. The open one. It has worked out fine so far,' replied Death moving towards the slightly ajar door on the left. 'Besides, there's a sign.'

'A clue?' said Reg moving forward.

'No an actual sign,' Death pulled off a sticky taped sign from the door and held it up.

'Oh.'

'All visitors and employees are required to sign in at

the security office for rigourous identity checks. Signed Dr Malcolm Pendelbury, Chief Security Officer,' said Death reading the sign aloud. 'Oh and there's a smiley face wearing a pair of glasses at the bottom. Never mess with a smiley face, that's my motto. And it's been laminated, so it must be important.'

'Actually they're called emoticons, not smileys,' said Bostock informatively, as he followed Death through the door.

Dr Malcolm Pendelbury and Dr Victoria Kloosterman shared a long, passionate, and somewhat haphazard kiss. It involved a lot of bumbling attempts to connect their mouths, including amongst others; a couple of head bumps, a clash of teeth, and the kissing and over exuberant sloppy licking of cheeks, chins, and noses. In their defence this had little to do with their inexperience in such endeavours (an inexperience which they had both spent many years developing). It had more to do with their present predicament. Dr Malcolm Pendelbury and Dr Victoria Kloosterman were locked in a cramped dark cupboard, with their hands tied firmly behind their backs. And lets face it, under such circumstances even the most ardent kissing aficionado would struggle with lip connection. After a particularly hard tooth bang they stopped for a breather.

'Wow! How did that happen?' asked Dr Victoria Kloosterman, whilst trying to rub off the excess saliva on her chin with her shoulder.

'Well it's probably a case of testosterone mixed with the pheromones released due to the dangerous situation we are both in,' explained Pendelbury. 'Neurologically speaking, the adrenaline release caused by recent events has most likely left us slightly prone to such chemical imbalances. Of course, that is just one aspect of it. We should also consider at what stage of your menstrual cycle you are, and then there's the attraction of physical features to consider, such as the popularity of a symmetrical face. And genealogical patterns should never be overlooked.'

'Oh.' Victoria had personally thought it had been due to the cupcakes she always brought him. She'd always believed that the way to a man's cardiac system was through his dietary tract.

'Yes. I wrote a thesis on it.'

'You did?'

'Yes. I was interested in Zena the Warrior Princess at the time and wondered if I could increase my chances of getting with her through the application of science. Of course, the release of the chemicals testosterone and oestrogen has more to do with lust than love; combined with norepinephrine, adrenaline in layman's terms, it greatly increases your chances,' said Pendelbury, who had apparently never heard of the concept of killing the mood. 'The chemicals that give us the sensation of love are oxytocin and vasopressin. I attempted to artificially produce them with the aid of prairie voles. Interestingly, oxytocin and vasopressin are usually at higher levels after coitus.'

'Hey don't get ahead of yourself, mister!'

'Oh no. I wasn't suggesting...' Pendelbury blushed deeply, but luckily for him it was too dark to see. 'Erm. Well, anyway. I never got that far with Zena the Warrior Princess to put my theory to the test.'

'Well if it's in the name of science.'

Victoria kissed him passionately on the ear before finding his mouth.

Reg and Eleri entered the security office behind Death and Bostock. The room somehow appeared too large for its purpose. In the mind, security offices are supposed to be small cramped rooms, containing an elongated desk in front of a bank of monitors and space for little else. This room did have the obligatory elongated desk and a line of monitors but it also had plenty of space for a lot more as well. It was at least fifty foot from one end to the other, and half as wide. The only furnishings other than the desk and monitors were five grey-metal double doored cupboards against the left wall, a potted rubber plant called Henry; as a sign on the pot informed them, and three swivel chairs; one of which lay overturned.

'Looks like there was a struggle,' remarked Eleri pointing to the overturned chair. 'And there's a half eaten cupcake, so what ever happened here probably happened suddenly.'

Death picked up the cupcake and examined it carefully before taking a bite.

'Death! That could be evidence! A clue.'

'It's very tasty evidence,' said Death, his mouth half full of cupcake. 'Oh look at that, they were armed with nunchucks after all. And what appears to be a broken mop with an elastic band taped to the handle. Reg you took a Vengeance Angel course on advanced weaponry, what do you make of it?'

Reg walked over to the desk where the weapons had been left. He had infact taken several night classes in an attempt to achieve his dream of becoming a Vengeance Angel. One of his favourite subjects had been advanced weaponry, although it had been mostly theory rather than practical, well for him anyway. His instructor had informed him that he "...was not to touch anything" after a minor incident involving a magnesium incendiary compound and the loss of the instructors eyebrows. Nevertheless he was quite sure how this weapon would be put into practice.

'Well comrade, it would appear to be a multi-attack recoiling striking device. The elastic band would enable you to take on multiple enemies at once. Like so.'

Reg put his hand through the elastic band and took a swing. The mop sprang back sharply, knocking over a desk lamp before striking him in the ear.

'Of course, mastering an advanced weapon like this would take months of training,' said Reg his teeth gritted against the pain.

'Ah yes, I can see that. So how do the nunchucks work?' asked Death hiding his smirk.

'Shhh. Did you hear that?' Pendelbury whispered, removing his mouth from Kloosterman's chin.

'Hear wha...' The crash of the lamp stopped her question mid-sentence. 'Help! We're in here!'

The hollow metallic echo of Kloosterman's yells filled the security room.

'Someone's in the cupboard,' said Eleri moving towards the source of the yells.

'Wait!' said Death. 'It might be a trap.'

'Someone in a cupboard yelling help. What sort of trap is that? I'm guessing surprise ninja ambush is out.'

'All the same we'd better arm ourselves. Reg grab those nunchucks. Bostock take the multi-attack recoiling striking device.'

Bostock looked at Death, confusion spread across his face.

'The broken mop.'

'What about me?' asked Eleri, looking around the room for something suitable to hit someone with. 'Shouldn't I be armed as well? And don't pull any of that you're a woman business.'

'You've got your pen,' said Death grinning.

'If you say the pen is mightier than the sword, I will stick the proverbial pen so far up your... Well lets just say you'll be grateful I haven't got a sword!'

'Everybody get ready to charge,' said Death placing his hand on the cupboard's handle.

'Hold up comrade,' said Reg stopping Death. 'I've just thought of what type of trap it might be. The cupboard could be rigged to explode. You know C4 and all that. They talked about it on my course.'

'That's highly unlikely,' responded Death, carefully removing his hand from the handle. 'New plan! Eleri, Bostock, with me in the strategic position of behind the desk. Reg you open the door.'

'Why me?'

'How many times do I have to go through this? You're already dead, and this suit is a tailor-made Armando Vespucci. It's irreplaceable.'

Bostock turned to Death as they crouched down behind the desk for cover.

'You don't think it'll explode do you? I don't know how much protection this desk will actually give us. Allowing for blast radius and considering our proximity to the detonation. From even a small amount of C4, I'd calculate we'd be a mural on the wall behind us.'

'Relax. It's not rigged to explode. I'm pretty sure the people inside would tell us if it was. They'd get blown up too.'

'So why are we hiding behind this desk?'

'I couldn't resist seeing the look on Reg's face as he opens the door expecting it to explode,' replied Death with a grin.

Reg pulled open the cupboard sharply and dived for cover as the metal door gave a slow creaking clank as it swung ajar. Satisfied that there was no accompanying loud bang, he peered inside to be greeted by the faces of Pendelbury and Kloosterman.

'They're scientists not ninjas,' announced Reg with his discovery.

'Are you sure?' asked Death from behind the desk.

'Well they're wearing white coats and one of them is a woman. Do they have female ninjas?'

'Of course they do. Otherwise there would be no baby ninjas.'

Pendelbury looked up at Reg from his cramped sitting position in the cupboard. Suspicion written across his face. Next to him sat Kloosterman her face was more a picture of embarrassment. With her ruffled hair and smeared lipstick it was quite obvious what she'd been up to. It was so embarrassing. Getting caught in the supply cupboard with someone. Even being tied up seemed little in the way of an excuse. In fact being tied up could be construed as even worse to a perverted mind and by the look of him the guy who had caught them had that sort of mind. What would her mother say? Kloosterman tried to sidle further away from Pendelbury but the cramped conditions provided little achievable distance. Feeling herself blush she ducked her head down. Pendelbury was the first to speak.

'How did you get in here? You can't just come waltzing in. There are procedures you know. There are three questions to answer. And a visitor log to fill in to get your passes.'

'The door was open,' explained Reg. 'I did knock.'

'Well very well, seeing as you're already in here, can you untie us? You can answer the security questions after.'

Death appeared beside Reg.

'We can't do that sorry. Besides it looks as if you're comfortable enough,' said Death indicating Pendelbury's lipstick covered face.

'Well if you're not here to rescue us, what are you doing here?'

'We are here to get the plague you stole.'

'Oh.'

'Yes oh. Now the way I see it there are two options.

One, you can answer our questions and we'll leave you in this cupboard. Or...'

'You're going to leave us tied up in here?'

'Yes. Or...'

'You'll never get us to talk. Nothing you can do will ever make us give up the information entrusted to us,' interrupted Pendelbury, a stubborn look of resolve on his face.

'Or,' continued Death ignoring the outburst. 'We can leave you tied up in this cupboard with that angry wasp I saw outside. What's it going to be?'

Pendelbury turned to Kloosterman, the two mouthed words between themselves before Pendelbury turned back to Death.

'We'll talk.'

'Good choice. Who else is in the building?'

'Just us and Professor Maximillian Kloch.'

'Nobody else, in a large facility like this?'

'Of course not.'

'Why of course not?' asked Death slightly confused by Pendelbury's declaration.

Pendelbury gave a sigh. 'Because they are showing *Hawk the Slayer* and *The Beastmaster* as a double bill in the local cinema complex of course.'

'Right. Of course,' said Death rolling his eyes. 'So where is Kloch?'

'In the basement. His private quarters.'

'And the plague is with him right?'

'Yes,' replied Pendelbury reluctantly.

'How do we get to this basement?'

Pendelbury deliberately closed his lips, pressing them tightly together, indicating he was not going to say anymore.

'How do we get to the basement?' repeated Death.

Pendelbury defiantly shook his head, his lips still firmly closed.

'Reg get the wasp!'

Pendelbury nervously watched as Reg slowly turned to leave.

'Okay, okay you win. You take the elevator over in the corner.'

'Thankyou,' said Death closing the door.

'Wait!'

Death reopened the door.

Pendelbury nodded his head towards Kloosterman and raised an eyebrow suggestively.

'You couldn't loosen one hand could you?'

Death closed the cupboard and walked to the elevator. The doors opened immediately as he pressed the button and he stepped inside, Reg and Eleri close behind. Bostock hesitated at the entrance.

'Maybe I should stay and guard up here.'

'What from an angry wasp? I made that up you know, and the scientists stroke ninjas are tied up in the cupboard,' said Death his finger on that convenient button that holds the door open in most elevators. 'Come on. Besides we might need you.'

'Oh yes, my intellect will most probably be required.'

'I was thinking more in terms of a sacrificial lamb should something go wrong, but yes okay, we may need your intellect.'

'Just so you know, I really don't like elevators,' said Bostock reluctantly stepping into the lift.

'So why the lift phobia?' asked Death as the elevator began its juddering descent. 'Is it the confined space or the maybe thought of plunging to your death? Or both, plunging to your death in a confined space?'

'You're not helping matters!' said Bostock through clenched teeth; his pallor visibly fading and a single bead of sweat appearing on his temple.

'I didn't realise I was supposed to.'

'Can we change the subject?'

'Lift phobia is called Otisaphobia, isn't it?' asked Death.

'No it's called Angkatphobia. And can we please change the subject.'

'I know, is it the fear that someone will break wind and you'll get the blame?' asked Death deliberately ignoring the Professor's request.

'Angkatphobia is strange isn't it. It's like a fear of flying. Before those Wright brothers invented those mechanical death traps, there was nothing to fear,' said Reg. 'I've often wondered what people with lift phobias feared before elevators were invented.'

'They were just normal,' explained Death. 'They didn't have any irrational fear of dying in a heap of twisted metal, if the cable suddenly snapped.'

Bostock groaned and slumped quivering into the corner.

'We're here,' announced Death as the elevator jerked to a stop. 'Pity really, I enjoyed that. But I suppose there is always the ride back!'

Unsurprisingly, Bostock was the first to exit the elevator. Springing past the others he took two deep and mostly pointless gasps of air.

'Ah, so it's a phobia of confined space,' said Death knowingly, giving Bostock a derisory pat on the shoulder as he stepped past him into Kloch's private quarters. 'I fear the plague may have already been relocated.'

'Why?' asked Reg, as he followed Death into the room. 'Oh.'

Reg stopped mid-stride as he noticed Kloch slumped in his wheelchair, his shirt blood-soaked.

'Is he dead?' asked Eleri joining them.

Death moved forward. 'Nope.'

'Are you sure?'

'Yep. I'm pretty good at this alive or dead stuff.'

Kloch opened his eyes, causing Reg to jump back and

adopt a stance which made him look a bit, but not entirely, like a martial arts expert.

'I'm Death.'

'I see they've moved with the times and ditched the whole black cloak look,' said Kloch with a slight cough, causing a fleck of blood to appear on his lips.

'Now that's what I call smart!' said Death towards the others.

'Am I dead? I don't feel dead. I somehow imagined it would be less painful.'

'No you're alive.'

'Oh good. I think I may have done something a bit stupid.' Kloch gave a groan of pain and closed his eyes for a brief moment before continuing. 'I may have stolen a deadly plague and then inadvertently lost it. Well, let it get stolen at least.'

'We know.'

'Yes I guess that's why you're here. Pendelbury and Kloosterman, are they okay? Kloch rose slightly with his sudden thoughts of concern for his colleagues' well-being, but pain forced him to slump back into his chair.

'They're fine,' reassured Death, presuming that Pendelbury and Kloosterman were the two scientists still locked in the cupboard upstairs. 'Eleri phone an ambulance. Now Professor Kloch, while you're waiting for medical assistance to arrive, why don't you tell us everything you know?'

'Who are you?'

'We're an elite team sent by the Heavenly Realm to retrieve the plague,' answered Death ignoring Eleri's snort at the term elite.

'I was tricked by Dr Laura Welsh and Dr Wolfgang Hissel. I only wanted to find a cure for the plague. So God would have no power over us. It sounds so stupid now, but you must believe me. And now, now it is gone. Oh dear, what have I done?'

'Calm down, we're the best of the best and if anyone can find the plague, we can. Now just tell us what you know.'

Kloch took a deep breath. 'Dr Welsh thinks she can use the plague to extort money but, but Hissel is going to double cross her! I heard him talking to some other party on the phone. He was taking instructions from someone else. I don't think Dr Welsh is aware of it. She was in the laboratory when he made the phone call. He is going to detonate the bomb regardless!'

'Bomb? What bomb?'

'That's why they came here. They needed my facility to safely transfer the plague. They transferred it into a cylinder rigged with some sort of detonary device. I saw it. She passed it to Hissel in front of me, they thought I was dead. I have been such a fool!' Kloch reached out and grabbed Death's sleeve. 'You must stop them!'

'We intend to.'

'Good.' Kloch briefly slipped into unconsciousness then came back around with a jerk. 'He intends to destroy the church. His target is Rome!'

Death turned towards the others. 'Then they have taken the plague to Rome.'

'No, you don't understand. The plague is airborne!'

'Yes we know.'

'Boratramontana,' whispered Kloch, his breathing shallow.

'What?'

Maximillian Kloch sighed, shut his eyes and fell into deep unconsciousness.

'I don't think we'll get anymore out of him,' said Death. 'Did anyone catch that last bit?'

'Boratramontana,' replied Reg confidently.

'Yes, but any idea what he was trying to say?'

Reg shrugged.

'Professor? Any ideas?'

'No sorry. Although my understanding of linguistics leads me to believe the dialect and pronunciation could be of Latin origin,' suggested Bostock. 'Other than that no immediate thoughts.'

'Well I guess that explains why they left the clues anyway. They obviously wanted to set the Galileists up as scapegoats. While we were busy chasing after the Galileists they were able to carry out their plans.'

'I suppose so,' said Reg. 'But why did Welsh and Hissel arrange to meet us if they had no intention of handing over the plague all along?'

Eleri and Death looked at each other sharply.

'It's a trap!' They replied in unison.

Chapter 20

Jenny and Norris entered the echoing courtyard of the Bargello Palace. The reverent hushed voices of visitors whispered through its numerous open archways and their footfalls accompanied them in a muted symphony of passage. Rising high above them stood the galleries, casting the inner courtyard in murky cooling shadow. The galleries' weather worn grandeur was fronted with carved stone plaques of families, their names faded away with the passage of time. Norris may have wondered when mankind had taken its turn from such beauty in favour of featureless monoliths that scar the modern cities. But he didn't; appreciating architecture 101, is a non compulsory course when saving the human race from a deadly plague.

'Right we need to get onto the roof.'

'Well I suppose we'd better use the stairs then,' said Jenny pointing to the two flights of stone steps that led to the upper galley from the courtyard.

Her pronouncement may have been taken as sarcasm from someone else, as the stairs appeared to represent the most obvious and certainly only option, but Jenny being a good Angel rarely used sarcasm. Of course, she also possessed a pair of wings, which opened up the possibilities of ascent considerably. On this occasion however, with so many people milling around, subtlety appeared to be the order of the day. So Norris and Jenny joined the wingless masses and climbed the stairs.

Reaching the top they walked across the upper level gallery until Jenny stopped at a narrow arched door.

'It's this way,' she announced pushing open the door.

'You sure?'

Jenny pointed to a "no admittance" sign and walked through. Norris gave a shifty glance to the left and right before following her through the door. Beyond the door a set of stone steps lead up towards the roof, the surrounding walls laced with cobwebs. The door closed behind Norris leaving them in complete darkness. Their shoulders brushed each side of the wall as they ascended the narrow stairwell. Using their hands to follow the wall as a guide, they cautiously began their stumbling climb upwards.

'I can't see anything,' complained Norris after a slight trip on one step.

'Well I can see everything.'

'Can you?'

'Of course. I'm using Angel vision.'

'Really?'

'No silly. I'm just as visually impaired as you, and no amount of carrots is going to help.'

'So how do you know we're going the right way?'

'Because we're going up.'

'Oh yer,' said Norris spitting out a bit of cobweb that had found its way into his mouth.

'Shh we're here,' said Jenny.

A slight crack of light framed a small door in front of them.

In a brilliant design flaw, the door opened inwards, forcing them to take two precarious steps backward in order to open it.

Each side of the Bargello Palace surrounding the open courtyard far below had its own separate roof. The individual roofs intersected and crossed over each other, confusing the eye like an M.C. Escher lithograph. An effect increased by the terracotta tiled roofs, each rising to an individual apex, separate from each other in such an irrational way that even a Scandinavian architect would have difficulty justifying it.

Behind them in one corner stood the bell tower; rising majestically into the pale blue Florentine sky. Its position amiably placed to allow a free line of sight of the busy street below (for any *would be* disgruntled crackpot with a high powered rifle).

At the far end, away from the entrance that Jenny and Norris had emerged through, stood Dr Welsh. In her hand she held a brown manilla envelope. Jenny and Norris walked slowly towards her, following the walled edge of the roof. Their stumbling steps clattered on the angled tiled roof which ended too close to the turreted wall to provide a decent walkway.

'That doesn't look like the plague in her hand,' whispered Jenny as they made their hindered way across the roof.

'It's probably the instructions of where to find it. It's how this kind of thing always works,' explained Norris knowledgeably.

He'd seen enough films and television programmes to know exactly how this sort of shady exchange worked. Granted they usually took place in carparks late at night, and involved raincoats, torches, and deep husky whispering voices.

'That's close enough,' said Dr Welsh as they neared.

'Have you got the plague? Norris asked in a deep husky voice.

'What?'

Norris coughed to clear his throat.

'Have you got the plague?'

'What?' Dr Welsh leaned forward to hear better.

'The plague. Have you got the plague?'

'Okay come a bit closer.'

Norris duly took a few steps closer.

'Have you got the plague?'

'This will tell you where it is hidden,' said Dr Welsh

holding up the envelope. 'Have you got the money?'

Norris held up his own manilla envelope containing Bostock's bogus formula for life itself.

'Wait. What money?' asked Norris.

'The money for the plague! What is this?' demanded Dr Welsh taking a step back. 'Where's the money?'

'We don't have any money. We've got the formula for life itself. Just as you asked. Look, see,' said Jenny taking the envelope from Norris and waving it.

'The exchange was supposed to be for twelve point four billion pounds in various denominations including pesos.'

'I don't suppose you'll take a cheque?' asked Norris hopefully.

'Do you take me for a fool?'

'No, but somebody does,' declared Death appearing beside her. 'Reg grab her!'

Reg took hold of Dr Welsh from behind holding her arms firmly behind her back.

'I'll take that thankyou,' said Eleri springing forward and snatching the envelope from Dr Welsh's hand.

'We had a deal! Where's my money?' screamed Dr Welsh in a frenzy as she struggled with Reg's hold. 'I want my pesos!'

Death moved forward, his face close to hers. The more friendly welcoming approach that the Human Transition Department had adopted over recent years disappeared. This was the serious Death.

'Now listen to me. Heaven doesn't do deals with terrorists. You don't get the secret of life itself, you don't get any money, even with the favourable exchange rate of pesos to the pound sterling, and you certainly don't get any virgins.'

Death stepped away from the subdued Dr Welsh.

'But we had a deal, for the money,' said Dr Welsh twisting her head to face Jenny.

'The deal, although extortion is probably a better word for it, was for the secret of life itself,' said Jenny.

'What do I need that for? I'm immortal. He promised me immortality for my help.'

'He? Kloch?' questioned Jenny.

'Hah! No. Bacchaus. Lord of the Underworld.'

'Bacchaus is involved in this?' asked Jenny nervously looking around as she spoke. 'What's going on? What has Bacchaus got to do with the Galileists?'

'The Galileists have been set up as scapegoats,' said Bostock, stepping forward from the rear. 'While we were chasing them, Dr Welsh here, and her partner Dr Hissel, could get away with their own plans. Isn't that right?'

'Dr Hissel, my partner! Don't make me laugh. You'll find his body in a train compartment somewhere between Switzerland and Northern Italy. My partner in this, shall we say, will remain anonymous. But let's just say Bacchaus introduced us. Now enough of our little chat, let me go or my partner will release the plague.'

'Oh I'm afraid we won't be letting you go,' said Death. 'See your partner in all this has double crossed you too. He has no intention of returning the plague. That's the trouble with dealing with Bacchaus. He's a demon. And demons don't have a great reputation when it comes to honesty. Bacchaus lied.'

'You lie!'

'No they lied. They intend to release the plague anyway. There is no money. You've been set up just like the Galileists. That's why the exchange was for the secret of life itself. It's an impossible request. You are not immortal, he has tricked you. Help us find the plague.'

'No. Bacchaus has given me immortality. You offer me nothing.'

'We offer you a chance of redemption and salvation.

Trust us. It's not too late to save your soul,' implored Jenny.

Dr Welsh stamped down on Reg's foot, causing him to yell, hop, and most significantly loosen his grip on her. With a duck and twist she broke free and leapt onto the walled edge of the roof.

'Oh great! Some Vengeance Angel you make,' said Death shaking his head at Reg.

'She took me by surprise!'

Dr Welsh glanced over her shoulder down to the street below, even with her promised immortality the height made her feel giddy.

'Wait,' said Jenny holding out her hands with her palms raised.

'Stay back!' commanded Dr Welsh.

'We can help you. It's not too late.'

'Too late?' Dr Welsh threw her head back laughing. 'Too late for what? You cannot offer me anything. I am immortal.

'No you're not,' said Jenny taking a step forward.

'Stay back. Bacchaus promised I will live forever, never ageing, never growing old. I have sold my soul for immortality'

'It's amazing what some people will do to beat the seven signs of ageing,' said Death casually. 'I mean don't they realise you can get a cream for that.'

'Bacchaus lied to you,' said Jenny ignoring Death's comment. 'Nobody can provide you with immortality. Immortality is only possible in the eternal afterlife. He tricked you, that's what he does. Come down, away from the edge and we can talk. It's not to late to seek mercy, you can help us.'

'I don't think so.'

Dr Welsh turned and leapt from the parapet. With her limbs flailing wildly in her freefall and her clothes fluttering around her, Dr Welsh made the rapid descent to the street below. She'd show them, they'd never catch her now. She was immortal. The fools! She let out a ringing laugh, which ended abruptly with a dull squelching thud.

Dr Welsh stood up. Immortality certainly did feel weird, almost ethereal. She looked down at her body, all twisted and broken. Oh dear.

The quiet voice of conscience inside her spoke. 'Told you,' said Laura. 'Oh shut up,' snapped Martha.

The others joined Jenny looking over the parapet at the scene below.

'Soul Sellers Department,' said Death, pointing to the shadows. 'Those guys even give me the creeps.'

The others all followed Death's gaze. The sun-cast shadows on the street below began to move, darkening and twisting into loosely formed humanoid shapes. A low deep moan sounding their arrival.

'What's happening?' asked Norris, his mortal status preventing him from viewing the scene as the others did.

'Trust me comrade, you don't want to know,' said Reg.

The dark shadowy shapes, now fully formed, began surrounding Dr Welsh's soul.

'No it's not fair,' she cried backing away from the shadows. 'We had a deal.'

'We call them wraiths,' said Death. 'They are the darker side of the Death Department. Nobody really ever talks about them. They deal with people who sell their souls, where no judgement is required. They work directly from Hell.'

The wraiths grasped at Dr Welsh's soul with their crooked limbs, their mouths gaping wide with heart stilling wails. Then, as one, they tore forward ripping at her ethereal being and dragging it with them back into the shadows. Dr Welsh gave one last pitying scream, then disappeared.

'That was awful,' said Reg shuddering. 'Those, er things, are horrible.'

'Yep,' said Death. 'They really put a dampener on the Christmas parties.'

'I think we should perhaps leave now,' suggested Eleri. 'Before the authorities arrive. It might be difficult to explain what an Angel, Death and a couple of souls are doing standing on the roof of the Bargello.'

Chapter 21

Eleri opened the manilla envelope she'd taken from Dr Welsh and pulled out the letter inside. The others gathered eagerly around her standing on the deck of Norris' yacht.

'What does it say?' asked the Professor.

Eleri paused, reading ahead before reading it aloud to the others; perhaps due to some journalistic instinct of finding a scoop.

'I have already given you enough clues to find the plague. But I will provide you with one final riddle to help you on your way. In Lyon I is next to Rome. Where eagles don't fly but lions do roam.'

'Is that it?' said Reg despondently. 'After all this, just another clue.'

Death took the letter from Eleri and checked both sides carefully, even holding the letter up to the sun to see if any secret message, might be found through some type of water mark.

'Nothing,' he said finally. 'Any ideas Prof?'

'Not immediately,' admitted Bostock.

'This makes no sense at all,' said Jenny. 'Why would he even bother giving us more clues? If he intends to release the plague anyway, then there is no reason to give us more of these riddles.'

'Because he's playing a game with us. He's mocking us,' said Eleri.

'Well mocking us or not, it's all we've got to work on right now,' said Death. 'In Lyon I is next to Rome. Where eagles don't fly but lions do roam.'

'Wait. Read it again!' asked Bostock.

'In Lyon I is next to Rome. Where eagles...'

'No, not that bit. The bit about enough clues.'

'I have already given you enough clues to find the plague.'

'Of course,' said Bostock hitting the palm of his hand against his head. 'It's a respondissent!'

'A what?'

'It's what we commonly refer to in the Angelic Times' Crossword Puzzlers' Society as a respondissent clue.'

'A what?' asked Death.

'It's a clue with two possible answers. Many years ago there was a crossword compiler called Ettin. Oh, and what a tricky bugger he was! Even today society members speak his name with hushed voices. His crosswords were devilishly fiendish. You see many of his clues would have two possible answers, both fitting perfectly. It wasn't until you were halfway through that you realised your error and would have to start right from the very beginning. Ruffled a few feathers I can tell you.'

'As much as I'm enjoying you regaling us with this tale, I must ask. What has this got to do with us?' asked Death.

'Don't you see? No of course you don't. The clues we've received. They are perfect respondissent clues. Our quarry has told us so.'

Bostock's explanation was greeted with blank faces. The sort of blank faces that you would get trying to explain the inner workings of the modern combustion engine, in Latin, to a Neanderthal man who still thinks fire is a pretty neat thing. Needless to say they didn't quite understand.

'Here,' said Bostock, pointing to the relevant part of the letter and reading it aloud. 'I have already given you enough clues to find the plague. He's telling us we already have everything we need to find the plague.'

'Nope. Still don't get it.'

'The clues he's already given us have a sort of double meaning. Two answers. The other possible answer will lead us to the plague.'

'Really? Brilliant! So what is the other answer?'

'Oh I don't know that.'

Bostock looked around at the disappointed faces surrounding him.

'Don't worry. I will solve this puzzle or I'm not the reigning Angelic Times' Crossword Puzzlers' Champion, four years running.'

'That's the spirit comrade,' said Reg tapping Bostock on the back. 'You are the reigning champion I take it?'

'Yes.'

'Okay, just checking.'

'Right!' said Death clapping his hands together. 'Let's see if we can get the plague! Okay, that didn't come out quite right. Jenny, Eleri and Reg help the Prof here solve this double clue thing. Norris, point the boat to the north-west. We're going to make the jump to open waters.'

'Where are we heading?' Norris asked, trying to give the impression that their direction might make some difference to his nautical expertise.

'The Adriatic. I hear it's nice this time of year. And should we fail in our task, signalling the demise of mankind, I'd kind of like to try and get a bit of a tan before the end.'

'Aye, aye,' said Norris in a voice he thought sounded nautical, and headed for the helm. He had grown accustomed to Death's ways. He knew that in spite of his nonchalance, Death always had an intricate plan. Granted it usually involved stumbling along relying on blind luck. But it was a plan, well of sorts, and it had worked for them before.

Below deck, Reg, Eleri, Jenny, and Bostock crowded

around the table studying the clues written on scraps of paper from Eleri's notebook. As an academic the Professor had long since trained his body to fully function without the inconvenience of engaging his brain. Thereby allowing him to continue his intense concentration and focus on the problem at hand. He hated wasting additional brainpower on mundane daily routines; such as making tea, drinking tea and the eventual and inevitable heading down the shops for more tea. This concept was also used by Albert Einstein who owned several sets of the same clothes, so he would not have to expend additional brainpower thinking about what to wear. However, Bostock had taken this idea one stage further and could even hold entire conversations on numerous topics without ever once consulting his brain.

After two cups of tea and a stimulating conversation about the role of tartan patterns in Scottish clan history Bostock looked up, nodding his head with a minute side to side motion as he mentally ran through the puzzle. Finally convinced his theory was correct he drew the attention of the others with an artificial cough.

'I think I've solved part of the clue,' announced Bostock.

'You have?' asked Jenny. 'Which part?'

'This bit from the poem we found in Huey Rousso's second house.' Bostock held up one of the scraps of paper and read aloud. 'Behind the greatest of men secrets do hide. In part the root of all evil turns to entry. Ireanus' mistake does an answer provide. But the shape of these words are also the key. Inside pushy lock the clue to see.'

'You've solved it?'

'Not all of it, just the line, *in part the root of all evil turns to entry.*'

'I was working on that bit,' said Reg, a slight timbre

of disappointment in his voice. 'The root of all evil is capitalism right?' he added in an attempt to get some recognition for solving it too.

'Well I suppose some people could look at it that way,' responded Bostock. 'Although I have a different answer.'

'Different how?' asked Reg.

'Mine is right,' replied Bostock. 'In part the root of all evil. Now the root of all evil has traditionally been associated with avarice. One of the seven deadly sins. Then you've got turns to entry. If you turn around the letters in entry you get try en. Try the letters e and n with part of avarice. And you get a place name. A city to be more precise.'

'Are you sure we're supposed to solve this comrade? It seems very complicated!' said Reg.

'It's Venice!' said Jenny clapping her hands with excitement. 'If you use the v, i, c, and e in avarice and put in the letters e and n you get Venice.'

'Yes well we can all see that now,' grumbled Reg. He had been sure that the root of all evil had alluded to capitalism.

'Exactly. Venice,' said Bostock smugly. 'The letters in avarice, v, i, c, e also spell vice and having a vice is also considered being the root of all evil.'

'Are you sure though? It still seems pretty thin, surely there could be another answer?' Reg wasn't going to let go of his capitalism idea without a fight. 'See if the root of all evil is capitalism, then part of the root of all evil could be capital. As in maybe a capital city or something. Though I suppose Venice is probably the capital of something.'

'Capitalism is not the root of all evil.'

'So you say,' muttered Reg.

'The root of all evil is avarice,' continued Bostock. 'And the answer is Venice.'

'But you can't be sure.'

'Well the answer Venice sort of unlocked another part of the clue,' said Bostock.

'Which bit?'

'Inside pushy lock.'

'That was the keypad.'

'It's a respondissent clue remember? Two answers! Inside the words pushy lock is the name Shylock. It's Shakespeare again. Shylock is from the Merchant of Venice.'

'Well that confirms it,' said Eleri. 'The plague is being taken to Venice. We'd better tell Death and Norris.'

'Tell us what?' asked Death as he and Norris entered the quarters from the upper deck.

'Oh didn't see you there.'

Death always had a way of sneaking up on you.

'We're not sinking again are we?' asked Norris looking at the makeshift repairs on the side of the yacht.

'I've solved part of the clue.' The Professor paused waiting for congratulations. They never came.

'And?' asked Death.

'It's Venice,' said Bostock and quickly explained the answer.

'Good. Norris set a course for Venice!'

'Erm. Okay.'

Norris pulled out several charts and maps from one of the small cupboards surrounding the living quarters and selected one. He rolled it out on the table and began studying it, hoping he could convince the others he knew what he was doing. The main problem with finding your way at sea as far as Norris was concerned, was the lack of signposts. Sure you had your GPS, but satellite navigation didn't quite cut it at sea. No richly toned voice told you to take the next right after the albatross, or informed you when you'd reached your destination. A big chunk of land normally did that job. Finding your way at sea generally required maps and charts. Maps and charts that generally didn't give you any indication of where you were. They just told you useless stuff like water depth and prevailing wind directions; and wind direction was no substitute for a map that told you to follow the little yellow line till Prestatyn Caravan Park. Plus the open ocean, the high seas, had no Little Chef Service Stations to stop at for a break when you felt tired.

Finally Norris twisted the map to face the direction they wanted to go and pointed.

'It doesn't make sense,' said Eleri whilst Norris was carefully plotting their course. 'Why would he take the plague to Venice if he wanted to destroy the Church in Rome like Kloch claimed?'

'I don't know,' admitted the Professor. 'But the clue definitely leads us to Venice. It must have something to do with Boratramontana, what ever that means.'

'Boratramontana,' repeated Reg. 'Could it be Italian or even Latin? There's been a lot of that lately.'

'It does sound Italian,' agreed Jenny.

'Spago, means string,' added Reg.

'What has that got to do with Boratramontana?'

'Well it's Italian isn't it.'

'We don't even know if Boratramontana is definitely Italian yet.'

'Well if it is, it doesn't mean string.'

'What are you going on about Reg?' asked Bostock irritably.

'It's deduction, like in Sherlock Holmes. Once you eliminate the impossible, what ever remains, no matter how improbable, must be the truth. I am deducing. Boratramontana isn't string. Or spaghetti either. That's already two things it isn't.'

'It isn't ice cream either, that's gelato,' said Eleri with

a smirk, seeing the annoyance on Bostock's face. 'That's three things it isn't.'

'Right you are there comrade sister,' said Reg, writing down gelato in his notebook under the heading things it's not.

'We don't even know if it is Italian yet,' grumbled Bostock.

'Yes it is, gelato means ice cream, I remember,' said Reg.

'Not bleeding gelato. I'm talking about Bora-sodding-tramontana!'

'What did you say?' asked Norris looking up from the map. 'Bora what?'

'Boratramontana. It was Kloch's last word to us,' explained Bostock. 'Does it mean anything to you?'

'It might do. Well that first bit anyway,' said Norris pointing his finger at the chart. 'Bora is written on this chart. The Bora is a wind.'

'The Bora is a wind?'

'Yes. I do know how to read a sea going mariner's chart thingy. According to this we'll be following the trade wind called the Bora.'

Bostock quickly pulled the chart towards him and the others gathered around.

'Maybe, just maybe,' muttered Bostock, tracing the path of the wind across the chart with his finger. 'Yes here! The Bora is a wind that travels across the Adriatic through Venice to central Italy. It is intersected by another wind. The Tramontana, which travels from Northern Italy all the way to Rome. It's two words! The Bora and Tramontana.'

'See I was right. I knew it didn't have anything to do with string,' announced Reg.

'Of course,' said Eleri. 'Kloch said the plague is airborne! He's going to use the wind to spread the plague to Rome.'

'Not just Rome,' said Bostock. 'The Mediterranean has been described as the birthplace of all winds. Once it spreads into that system of winds it will be almost impossible to track. There will be no way to predict accurately where it will strike next in order to quarantine that area off.'

'Well we'd better get to Venice fast,' said Death. 'Norris get on the helm.'

'Yes,' said Norris, standing still.

'The helm is the steering wheel.'

'Right yes,' said Norris before bounding up the stairs to the deck.

'And Professor, no pressure but you'd better try and solve the rest of this clue, because the whole of civilisation as we know it is relying on you!'

Death joined Norris on the deck and sat down near the helm with his back against the rail. He rolled up his trouser legs to the knees and his sleeves to the elbows and looked up grinning at the sun. Above them the sail billowed with the rise and fall of a favourable wind as they headed towards Venice in a fine example of chance, rather than through Norris' nautical expertise.

'Couldn't we do a pan dimensional jump to Venice?' asked Norris.

'Don't think we really need to, we're not that far from Venice and we still need to solve the rest of the clue,' replied Death. 'Until we've got a more specific idea of where the plague is hidden then there's no need to rush. We seem to be making good speed anyway.'

'Did you know that the reason a ship's speed is measured in knots is because they used to drop a rope over the side with knots tied at various intervals? So they could see how many knots distance they had travelled over a certain period of time and therefore work out how fast they were travelling.'

'Yes.'

'Oh.'

'So how many knots are we travelling?'

'I don't know. I'm not sure how far apart I'm supposed to tie the knots on the rope.'

'Oh well. Nice day for the end of mankind though, don't you think?'

'Well I suppose.'

'Sure it is,' said Death. 'If the world as we know it is going to end, I'd much prefer it to be a sunny one. End of the world and drizzly rain, now that would be depressing.'

'Shouldn't we be doing something, you know more proactive?'

'We are being proactive. Bostock and the others are hopefully solving the rest of the clue and we are travelling to Venice at an undetermined rate of knots. There's not much more we can do at the moment, so I am proactively working on my tan.'

Below deck, Professor Bostock, Eleri, and Jenny sat around the table contemplating the clues before them. Reg had taken to pacing back and forth in a manner that he believed an intellectual might adopt, to see if it helped. It didn't.

'Okay so this line, *behind the greatest of men secrets do hide,*' said Bostock. 'I think the greatest of men must be like you suggested first of all Jenny.'

'You mean Jesus?' asked Jenny.

'Yes. But then it raises the question, what or who is behind Jesus?'

'Well I suppose you could say the Angels and Archangels are behind Jesus. Then there are the saints and apostles. The list goes on. There are just so many options.'

'Well let us see if we can narrow it down a bit. The Angels and Archangels are generally associated with God rather than Jesus, so I suppose we could start with the saints and apostles.'

'Okay. What about Ireanus he's a saint?'

'Well seems like as good a starting point as any.'

'I'll go ogle Ireanus again and see if there's something we missed the first time around,' said Jenny pulling out her phone.

'Yes go ogle Ireanus, and see what comes up,' agreed Bostock.

Damn it, thought Bostock. He'd used go ogle instead of google. Although, he had to admit the term was growing on him. It certainly made more sense than a spelling mistake of googolplex. He'd once read an article about a flange of gorillas that had apparently become more intelligent after spending time in close contact with a group of scientists. He couldn't help wondering if the reverse was also true, and the scientists had become slightly thicker.

'Oh it says here that Saint Ireanus was born in Lyon, France. What did the clue say about Lyon?'

'In Lyon I is next to Rome,' read Eleri aloud.

'But Lyon is in France. It is nowhere near Rome,' announced Reg knowledgeably.

'I suppose next to Rome could imply a closeness to the Church. Which Ireanus certainly is being a saint and everything,' suggested Jenny.

'Maybe there's a church or statue in Rome dedicated to Ireanus. There are a lot of churches in Rome,' said Reg.

'It says next to Rome not in Rome, but there could be a church just outside the city or a monument or, I don't know, something,' added Eleri.

'I'll check,' said Jenny.

'So Ireanus was French huh,' said Reg filling the silence while Jenny checked for churches, statues, and monuments surrounding Rome. 'I was totally hopeless at French in school. *Je mapel Reg*. I am Reg.'

'What?' Bostock looked at Reg sharply.

'I know hopeless. Three years and I only learnt to say I am Reg.

'Reg you've cracked it!'

'I have?' said Reg pulling up his trousers at the waistband.

'Yes you have! In Lyon. It's French! I is *je*. Put *je* next to Rome. Jerome! Behind the greatest of men secrets do hide, behind Jesus the saints. It's Saint Jerome! Jerome is the patron saint of libraries. And Venice must have a library.'

'Wait a second,' said Jenny. 'I just read something about Saint Jerome. Here! It says that it is generally regarded that Ireanus made a mistake in attributing the four apostles to the winged creatures in Ezekiel. A later interpretation made by Saint Jerome is considered the definitive in most modern texts.'

'Ireanus made a second mistake. Two mistakes two separate answers. The perfect respondissent clue,' said Bostock.

'It's here. The four Apostles Matthew, Mark, Luke, and John were each assigned to one of the winged creatures sitting at the side of God in the visions in Ezekiel 1:1-14. Ireanus and Jerome agreed on Luke and Matthew but not on Mark and John. Ireanus claimed John was represented by the winged lion and Mark the eagle. Jerome claimed it was the other way around.'

'The clue! Where eagles don't fly, but lions do roam!' exclaimed Reg.

'Exactly,' said Jenny. 'We're looking for the winged lion. And Jerome claims that the winged lion is Saint Mark.'

'Of course,' said Bostock. 'Saint Mark is the patron saint of Venice. The symbol of the winged lion is all over Venice.'

'Then we are getting close!' Jenny clapped her hands

together.

'Yes. But there are numerous representations of Saint Mark and the winged lion all over Venice. There must be something else in the clues to narrow it down.'

'But the shape of these words are also the key,' said Reg pointing to the poem. 'The words were written in a square.'

'The Piazza San Marco. Saint Mark's Square,' said Bostock only confirming what the others had already realised.

'Death! We've solved it!' shouted Reg to the upper deck.

Death and Norris rushed down from the deck into the crowded cabin.

'So what's the answer? Where's the plague?' asked Norris.

'Saint Mark's Square,' said Bostock and quickly explained the answer whilst giving himself the starring role in finding the solution.

'What about the other clue?' asked Norris when Bostock had finished. 'A plague in both your houses.'

'We haven't done that bit yet. But I'm guessing it's some sort of anagram giving us a precise location. Saint Mark's Square is a big area to find a small cylinder in. But we are getting there!'

'Well I hate to be the party pooper,' said Death. 'But we haven't got the plague yet. So let's not sacrifice the fatted calf before the fat lady sings, and all that. '

'Er who's piloting the boat?' interrupted Jenny.

Norris gave a quick look around the cabin, mentally accounting for everyone. Then, when his calculations were finally complete, he turned around wide eyed, and sprinted up to the deck.

Chapter 22

The companions stood upon the deck of Norris' yacht and looked out at the approaching city of Venice. Soon the terracotta tiled buildings of the surrounding islands became clearly visible, and with them the beauty of the seaward journey into Venice. Visitors to Venice can do little but stare at the wondrous and ingenious city, its grace apparent from the first moment it is viewed.

'The people who built Venice were pretty stupid if you ask me,' said Reg. 'Less than ten miles over there is perfectly good solid land. So where do they build? On water. I mean I'm no architect or builder, but even I know houses are supposed to be built on land. And then they complain and get all concerned that it's sinking. Well serves them right for being opulent show-offs.'

'Venice is actually built on a series of interconnected islands,' muttered Bostock.

'Well Manchester has more canals and proper ones too. You don't see gondolas going up and down them. They're a proper working man's canals for transporting goods from the factories.'

'Nobody uses the Manchester canals for transporting goods anymore,' said Bostock.

'Well obviously they use roads now, because the people who built Manchester were smart enough to build on solid land,' said Reg triumphantly, his point, whatever it was, being made.

'Well I think it's an incredibly romantic city,' said Jenny. 'With its gondolas passing softly under moonlit bridges and the mysterious masquerade balls.'

'Oh and don't forget Casanova,' gushed Eleri. 'The world's greatest lover.'

'Casanova had syphilis,' stated Death flatly. 'And I for one don't intend waiting around long enough to catch it. Norris head to the south, we can anchor up right next to Saint Mark's Square.'

'Won't we get in trouble for parking there?' asked Norris. 'I don't want to get any points on my license.'

'They're hardly going to be able to clamp us and right now I think a fine is the least of our worries. Trust me when saving mankind, illegal parking is not an issue.'

'I think we're in the right place,' said Eleri. 'Look!'

In front of the entrance to Saint Marks square stood two looming pillars. The western pillar was capped at its apex with a statue of the winged lion of Venice and Saint Mark, the low evening sun bathing it in a pale orange light.

'Pull up here,' said Death, indicating a nearby quay.

'That's for taxi boats only,' pointed out Norris.

'And paying customers. This is Italy remember.'

Death leapt athletically onto the wooden boarded dock, and was promptly confronted by a blustering official. With a fluid movement, Death pulled out a bundle of notes from inside his suit jacket and thrust them at the official. With the introduction of euros the blustering miraculously turned into smiles and several appreciative nods. Death waved to the others to follow him.

'Ah, I love Venice,' he sighed as the others made their way to join him on the quayside. 'Any luck with that final clue yet Professor?'

'Well I'm convinced it is an anagram. Trouble is a plague in both your houses has numerous options. Such as hairy tuna lubes goo up shoe. I feel I am getting very close with two of the options though. O thou plague by horses in au. Although of course au doesn't make sense.

And the other is O thou plague near his buoys, which does fit but doesn't quite help us solve anything. I was hoping that being here might provide some inspiration.'

'Has it?'

'Not as yet.'

'Doesn't thou mean you?' asked Eleri.

'Yes.'

'O you plague, it doesn't really fit does it. Shouldn't it be thine for your instead? O thine plague.'

'Well I'm allowing a bit of scope because it's an anagram. But also I think thou could be being used in this instance in reference to God, a sort of biblical prose sort of thing,' explained the Professor. 'Naturally, he could be just mocking us. The use of thou played two roles; to signify an inferior, or a love. He could be calling us an inferior.'

'Or a love,' said Death. 'Although I'm inclined to agree with inferior. I don't think we've got a love hate thing going on here.'

Interestingly, Professor Cobblers identified the use of thou to address an inferior in his 1998 work, *The Myth of Love and Romance*. Cobblers claimed that the use of thou as a precursor to the modern you has not two uses to designate you as either an inferior or as a love as previously believed, but only one; to address an inferior. Thereby undermining the use of thou in all romantic works. Furthermore, Cobblers states that this is proof that love does not exist and the use of thou is purely to trick an inferior into having sex with you. It should be noted that Professor Cobblers was going through a rather messy divorce at the time of publication.

'Okay let's split into groups, we can cover more ground that way,' said Death. Jenny and Norris have a look around the Doge's Palace and the Basilica, see if you notice anyone or anything suspicious.'

'Like what?' asked Norris.

'Well, like someone carrying a cylinder containing a deadly plague with a bomb attached. Or mime artists, can't trust those devious masters of movement either.'

'Got it! Terrorists carrying bombs or mimes,' said Norris eagerly. 'Which way is the Doge's Palace.'

'Come on,' said Jenny taking his hand and leading him away.

'Okay Reg, Professor, take a look around and see if anything inspires the solving of the remaining clue.'

'What if we happen to see any terrorists carrying bombs?' asked Reg.

'Then and only then can you come and get me. I'll be in that cafe over there. Come on Eleri, I'm going to introduce you to the best Kiwi fruit ice cream that money can buy.'

Death led Eleri to the cafe quarter surrounding the edge of Saint Mark's Square. Neat rows of tables and chairs providing a natural habitat for Venice's social elite, and holidaymakers. Giving the latter the perfect opportunity to regale family and friends with tales of extortionate coffee prices.

'I feel like everyone is looking at me,' complained Eleri. 'It's like they're judging me.'

'That's because they are. If you're not carrying this season's latest designer handbag then you're a social pariah.'

'I hate that.'

'Oh, it gets worse. The waiter will find you a seat according to his perception of your social standing.'

As if in a response to Death's somehow prophetic words a waiter appeared.

'Table for two? This way please.' The waiter led Death and Eleri to a prominent table far away from the bunched up holidaymakers. Eleri glowed with pleasure at her position amongst the Venetian elite.

'We didn't do so badly being seated here did we?'

'Actually, I'm two rows further back from when I came here on my own.'

'Oh.'

'Hey I'm not saying it's your fault. I think you look great.'

'Good.'

'But this suit is a taylor made Armando Vespucci though.'

'Hey!'

'Just saying that's all. It's how they are here. I'm not the one judging you for wearing an off the peg top.'

'Are you this charming to all your dates? Eleri blushed. 'Not that this is a date. We're here to save mankind. Why are we here? The cafe I mean, not the saving mankind bit, that's pretty self-explanatory.'

'We're here to enjoy the finest kiwi fruit ice cream you will ever taste.'

'Shouldn't we be finding the plague?'

'Right now Professor Bostock is probably the only one capable of solving the clue. And Norris and Jenny are out there looking for something suspicious.'

'Shouldn't we be looking for something suspicious too?'

'We are. Something suspicious is just as likely to find us while we're sitting here enjoying kiwi fruit ice cream, as we are of finding it. Plus we don't run the risk of bumping into any mime artists.'

Jenny and Norris stood to one side as a small tour group passed by them outside the Basilica. The guide's clear pronounced tone rose above the hubub of chatter in the piazza. 'The famous four horses atop the main entrance to the Basilica were eventually returned after being stolen by Napoleon's troops in...'

'It's really hard knowing what's suspicious and

what's not. If you ask me Italians have a natural talent for being suspicious. That's probably why they're so good at all that Mafia stuff,' remarked Norris.

'Maybe the problem is that whoever we're looking for is most likely trying not to look suspicious. So we should really be looking for someone that isn't actually suspicious.'

'Let's go back to the Doge's Palace then. There were loads of people not being suspicious there.'

Professor Bostock and Reg stood in the middle of Saint Mark's Square, surrounded by pigeons and tourists in equal measure.

'Found any inspiration yet comrade? asked Reg, after threatening a pigeon with physical violence if it didn't leave him alone.

'I know I'm close. A plague in both your houses has got to be an anagram. And I'm fairly sure it's going to start with O thou plague. But the rest is beyond me.'

'Well it's beyond me too. So far all the clues have been about Shakespeare and science. And to be honest comrade, neither are in my field of expertise.'

'That's it!' shouted Bostock, scaring off a bunch of pigeons and tourists alike. 'You've done it again! Reg you beautiful little man. Science! That's the key.'

'It is?'

'Don't you remember the anagram O thou plague by horses in au?

'You said au didn't make sense.'

'It's science. Au! It's the chemical symbol for gold, from the latin aurum. O thou plague by horses in gold!'

'Is that significant?'

'The entrance to the Basilica has four statues of golden horses on top of its entrance. I'd call that pretty significant. The plague is at Saint Mark's Basilica.'

'Which one is the Basilica?'

Bostock pointed to the most prominent building surrounding the square. 'That one!'

'Right time for action,' said Reg, pulling up his trousers at the waistband. 'You get Death and Eleri. I'll get Jenny and Norris.'

Death and Eleri were just scraping up the last remnants of liquidised kiwi fruit ice cream from their bowls as Bostock arrived. He brushed past the waiter who tried to seat him amongst the holiday makers.

'The plague is at the Basilica!' he announced loudly, much to the alarm of the surrounding customers.

'See,' said Death, taking his last mouthful of ice cream. 'As always, planned to perfection. Date over,' he added with a grin and a wink, that caused Eleri to resume her earlier blush.

'You solved the final clue?' asked Eleri, in an attempt to draw attention away from her blush.

'You see, the four horses,' said Bostock pointing across the square. 'A plague in both your houses. It's an anagram. O thou plague by horses in Au. Au is the symbol for gold. It is referring to the horses at the entrance to the Basilica.'

'Well let's get going then,' said Death, leaving a handful of euros on the table.

Death, Eleri and Bostock made the short journey across the square to the front of Saint Mark's Basilica, where the others stood waiting. High above the entrance stood four statues of horses in wild gallop.

'Okay then guys, let's find this plague,' said Death, more cheerfully than someone really should be when searching for a deadly plague, but easily forgivable when not fully versed in plague finding etiquette.

The companions spread out scanning the Basilica's ornate frontage, searching the various nooks and crannies that the Basilica offered as a suitable hiding place, and in one instance rifling through an elderly couple's holdall. The latter incident causing a great deal of disturbance, particularly when Reg announced he was looking for a bomb. After a few choice words and a handbag blow to the head, Reg returned the sandwich box; which to be fair, could have held a bomb rigged cylinder containing a deadly plague and not six cheese and pickle sandwiches and a chocolate orange club biscuit for dessert.

'This is hopeless comrades,' said Reg to Death and Bostock who were standing nearby looking up at the horse statues trying to see if the plague had been hidden up there.

'I think you're right,' agreed Death. 'If the plague was here we would have surely found it by now. Professor are you sure you've got the clue right?'

'O thou plague by horses in gold. It's got to mean the horses of the Saint Mark's Basilica.'

'They look more green than gold,' commented Norris, as he and Jenny joined the impromptu meeting.

'That's because they're bronze not gold,' explained the Professor.

'I thought they were supposed to be gold not bronze. Au is gold.'

'These are just bronze replicas. The original gold gilt statues are on display inside.'

Death gave Bostock a withered look.

Across from the Basilica a *decidedly not very suspicious at all* figure, paced slowly back and forth. Occasionally and very casually, he looked up from the phone call he was making, only briefly, then he buried his head, concentrating back on the pavement. He was perhaps the most unsuspicious figure you were likely to see, unless of course you knew he was a demon. Iscyrus watched as the companions entered the Basilica.

'They've gone inside,' Iscyrus reported to the phone's

recipient.

'Good. You have done well,' replied the voice on the phone.

Ceiling height has long been associated with wealth; the higher your ceiling the richer you are. As Death and the others entered Saint Mark's Basilica they paid little attention to the high domed ceiling that rose above them. If they had they would have surely concluded that Saint Mark had quite a few euros to his name.

'This way.' The Professor confidently led the party up a flight of stairs to the gallery where the gilt horses were displayed. A tour guide led a group from the annex as they arrived, leaving the companions alone in the room. The horses stood together with separate plinths beneath their feet, and surrounded by the wide arches in the brickwork that gave access the gallery.

'I would have thought they would have had security guarding these horses,' said Reg looking around.

'Someone is hardly going to stuff one of these up their jumper and run off with it,' said Bostock.

'Well Napoleon did!'

'Erm, about this plague we're looking for?' asked Norris.

'Yes?' replied Death.

'Would it be in a glass cylinder?'

'Yes it could be.' Death took a step towards Norris who had positioned himself to the rear of the horses.

'With some sort of bomb attached?'

'Yes.'

'And a countdown timer?'

'Yes,' said Death standing alongside Norris.

'I think I've found it.'

'I think you have,' said Death looking down at the bomb rigged cylinder.

'What do we do now?' asked Jenny.

'It's funny because now that we've finally found it,

the words run away spring to mind,' replied Death. 'Right well I guess we get it out of here first, before someone comes.'

'Sounds like a plan comrade,' said Reg.

'Yes it does, doesn't it,' said Death grinning. 'Right Reg, pick it up and put it under your coat.'

'Why me?'

'Really? Do we have to go through this every time?'

'Okay,' sighed Reg. 'I get it. I'm the Vengeance Angel and your suit is expensive. What if it explodes?'

'Relax. We've got plenty of time. There's twenty four hours on the timer. We'll just take it back to the boat and work out something from there.'

'Actually I think it's twenty four minutes,' said Eleri looking closely at the timer. 'Twenty three.'

When facing twenty three minutes till the end of the world, pointless declarations of love (considering the time involved) appear to be the order of the day. Such as declaring your undying love to the girl/guy sitting on the opposite table to you in the coffee shop. This is probably due to said time involved and the knowledge of not having to face the consequences afterwards, and is one of the main reasons why apocalyptic prophecies should always be regarded with caution. In some cases however, it just forces the individual to declare a love that they had been meaning to get around to for quite some time now. Norris was one such case.

'Jenny can I have a word with you in private?'

Norris took Jenny's hand and pulled her to one of the archways away from the others, idly turning over the engagement ring in his pocket as he led the way.

'Jenny, we've known each other for quite some time now and there's something I've been meaning to get around to. You said you thought this was a romantic setting, Venice that is. And I've been waiting to find a suitable setting to say what I'm saying. Not this bit but the next bit, after this.' Norris gulped. This was going wrong. It was taking too long, it wasn't supposed to be like this. It was supposed to be smooth, well rehearsed and most of all very romantic. No wait, most of all successful. Maybe he should just blurt it out, that was kind of romantic in a sort of spontaneous way. 'Jenny I love you and...'

'Come on you two,' said Death as Reg stuffed the cylinder under his coat.

'Norris I love you, but we only have twenty three minutes to save the world!'

Jenny gave Norris a quick kiss, turned and followed the others out.

'Bugger it!' cursed Norris and ran after them.

'Eighteen minutes, twenty eight seconds,' announced Reg as they left the Basilica.

Death looked at his pocket watch. 'I suggest we run. Reg.'

'Yes?'

'Don't drop it. Come on.' Death cut his way through the milling tourists, the others close behind and at a cautious distance from Reg.

The soft twinkling lights of Venice began to spring to life as dusk fell and the companions reached the quay. Crowds of tourists deciding how to spend their evening watched as the strange group dashed past, entirely oblivious to the danger they were in.

'Fourteen minutes, forty eight seconds,' reported Reg as they made their way onto the yacht.

'Norris get us to open water, where we can make a Pan Dimensional Jump,' shouted Death. 'I'm going to call Archangel Michael.'

Like a well oiled yet slightly defunct machine they loosened the moorings and set sail. The yacht left a bright white wake against the darkening sea as Venice and daylight were both left behind. Death standing on the prow dialled the Archangel's number.

'Moneypenny can you put me through to Archangel Michael, a direct line please,' said Death.

After a short delay Archangel Michael's voice came through.

'Hello Death. Good news I hope.'

'The plague is in our possession.'

'Excellent. Make a Pan Dimensional Jump to the Heavenly Realm and I will arrange for those boffins in Bio Hazard and Plagues to meet you on arrival.'

'We do have a slight problem. The plague has been transferred into a glass cylinder.'

'Oh yes that is a problem. You'd best transfer the plague into a safer container before bringing it back here.'

'Er, that isn't the slight problem bit sir. The cylinder also has a small bomb attached to it. And it's due to explode in about fourteen minutes.'

'Twelve minutes, and two seconds,' interrupted Reg, beads of sweat forming on his forehead as he held the cylinder at arms length.

'Twelve minutes,' repeated Death into the phone.

'One day Death we are going to have to discuss the meaning of the word slight.'

'I was kind of hoping you might have some sort of idea what we can do.'

'Well the words run away do spring to mind. Can you detach the bomb from the cylinder?'

'The bomb is inside the cylinder we can't access it without opening it and releasing the plague.'

'Oh that is unfortunately clever.'

'Yes I thought that too. I was wondering if you could have something ready at your end to neutralise the explosion.'

After a brief pause Archangel Michael spoke again.

'I'm sorry, but we can't risk a Pan Dimensional Jump with the plague in the precarious state it is in. If the plague

is released during the jump it would spread expeditiously. We cannot risk that, we've got to stick to procedure. I'm afraid you would appear to be on your own on this one.'

'I understand,' said Death, his heart sinking.

'I'm sorry Death. Goodluck.'

'Thankyou.' Death hung up the phone and called the others to join him.

'I hate being the bearer of bad news,' said Death, which was quite a strange declaration considering his chosen profession. 'But we have a slight problem. We can't make a Pan Dimensional Jump, it's standard procedure. The bomb is about to detonate in...'

Death looked at Reg.

'Nine minutes,' filled in Reg.

'Any ideas? Now is the time if you've got any.'

'Bacchaus must have planned this from the very beginning,' said Jenny. 'That's why we've been given all those clues. He wanted us to find the plague. It hasn't been about destroying humanity at all, it's been about destroying us. It's about revenge.'

The Professor looked closely at the cylinder.

'Well the bomb is of a very rudimentary design, if we could manage to cut that red wire there. We could disable it. We will need some sort of wire cutter of course.'

'We can use my swiss army knife! It's got a nifty little wire cutter attachment,' said Reg pulling out his knife from his pocket and nearly dropping the cylinder in the process.

'There is another problem. Once we open the cylinder to cut the wire we will release the plague into the air anyway. We need an airtight facility like the Galileist's laboratory.'

'Airtight!' exclaimed Death, snapping his fingers. 'We have got somewhere completely airtight. Isn't that right Norris?'

'My submersible!' said Norris. 'We can place the plague in my submersible.'

'You got it. It's an airtight plan, excuse the pun,' said Death grinning. 'Actually no, enjoy the pun.'

With claps on the back and cheers the companions congratulated each other.

'Well comrades we've saved the world again. With nearly eight minutes to spare,' said Reg laughing.

'Not quite,' said Bostock, who hadn't joined in the celebrations. 'I calculate that the extra internal pressure that would be created by even a small explosion within the submersible will fatally compromise its integrity.'

'So what does that mean?' asked Norris, worried it meant his submersible would be somehow damaged.

'It means that the submersible will not remain airtight once the bomb goes off. Granted if we submerge the vessel the surrounding water should slow the process but the plague will still eventually be released into the air.'

'What are you saying?' asked Jenny a worried look on her face.

'He's saying that one of us will have to go into the submersible with the plague and disarm the bomb,' said Death.

'But that's suicidal,' said Eleri.

'Yes it is.'

Reg slowly moved away from the others and opened the hatch to the submersible and placed the plague inside before turning to face them.

'I guess this is goodbye comrades,' he said solemnly.

'What are you talking about Reg?' asked Death.

'It's me. I'm the Vengeance Angel remember? It's my job on this mission, you know to do all the dangerous stuff. I'm the one who's going to take the plague down in the submersible with me and disarm the bomb.'

'Not this time comrade,' said Death. 'I'm responsible

for this. So step aside, I'm taking the plague.'

'No,' said Jenny. 'We're all in this together. We're all responsible.'

The others all nodded their agreement.

'We'll draw straws,' continued Jenny. 'And there's no point in arguing we haven't got the time. We'll let fate decide.'

Death paused for a moment. 'Very well. I guess it's the best way to solve this. Norris cut some rope into lengths.'

'Here use this,' said Reg passing Norris his treasured swiss army knife.

'Oh and Norris, make one piece shorter than the rest,' added Death.

Norris cut a piece of rope that he was fairly sure wasn't doing anything important, into lengths, placed the knife beside the submersible and passed the cut rope to Death.

'Okay who's first?' asked Death.

Eleri stepped forward and in the age old tradition pulled one of the pieces of rope from Death's hand.

'It's a long one,' said Death. 'Next?'

Reg stepped forward and pulled a rope length.

'Long,' said Death as Reg held up his chosen piece.

Reg looked around at his comrades with guilt. 'I'll take it.'

'We all decided to do it this way,' said Jenny patting Reg on the shoulder as she moved forward to take her turn.

'Long,' said Death as Jenny slowly pulled out her choice. 'Norris?'

Taking a deep sigh, Norris gripped an end of rope and pulled.

'It's the short one,' said Death.

'Hey I guess that's just my luck, huh,' said Norris a wry smile on his face.

'I can't let you do this,' said Reg defiantly. 'You're my comrade, my friend. I'll take the plague.'

'I've already killed you once before Reg, remember?' said Norris with a smile. 'You don't think I'll let you die because of me again do you?'

'Death, surely you must be able to do something? Anything? Bostock?' Reg turned to face the Professor, desperation in his eyes.

'There just isn't the time,' said Bostock shaking his head with remorse.

'Damn it!' Death cursed. 'We'll make a jump.

'No! We can't risk it,' said Norris firmly. 'It's done.'

The sound of the something large hitting the water broke their conversation. Turning they saw Jenny disappearing inside the submersible. Norris ran and jumped into the water just as she sealed the entrance. Norris desperately pulled at the seal in vain, then swam across to the porthole.

'Jenny! What are you doing?'

Jenny looked at Norris through the glass her words dulled by the enclosed submersible.

'I'm sorry. I couldn't let you do it. I'm your Guardian Angel after all,' she gave a bitter smile and moved to the ballast release lever.

'Don't you touch that Jenny. Jenny!'

Foam bubbled around the vessel as it began to sink down into the dark water, its lights illuminating the surrounding area. Norris gripped tightly at the porthole, following it under the water. His fingers whitened as he frantically pulled at the surrounding seal. Norris' lungs were beginning to burn as he sunk deeper. With a final effort he hammered his fist at the glass. Then her face was there looking out at him. He was losing his grip.

'Don't do this. I love you!' Foaming bubbles released with his words.

'I'm sorry,' mouthed Jenny, pressing the palm of her

hand to the glass. 'I love you.'

Norris pressed his hand to match Jenny's hand on the other side of the glass. For a brief moment they looked into each others eyes. Then Norris lost his grip and the submersible sank beneath him. He swam after it, the lights fading below. Then his lungs gave in. He floated in the water exhaling his remaining air, his body jerked with the last of his life giving oxygen. Then Death was there pulling him to the surface.

Reg and Eleri pulled Norris up onto the deck, Death following behind him. Norris turned towards Death his breathing shallow.

'You've got to get her! Make a jump or something.'

'It's too late. I'm sorry.'

'Maybe she'll make a jump out of there. She will won't she?' Norris looked at Death hopefully.

Death put his hand on his shoulder. 'She won't.'

'Time's up,' said Reg grimly, looking at his watch.

Norris sat on the deck in silence as the reality came crashing in. She was gone. He looked at the others, tears rolling freely down his face.

'I always knew I'd die for her. But I never realised I had nothing to live for without her.'

The others wanted to comfort Norris but they knew there was nothing they could say, so the five sat close together on the deck in silence, each with their own thoughts.

'Look,' said Eleri drawing their attention to the night sky.

A star suddenly flared brighter than any other in the black sky. Its aura lit up the surrounding area for one dazzling moment before leading a blazing trail across the dark blanket of night. Then it was gone.

'A shooting star,' she said solemnly.

Norris dropped his head. 'It was beautiful.'

Epilogue

Bugflug entered the private chambers of Bacchaus. Even for an optimist Bugflug was nervous today. It was the last day of his probation as personal secretary. After today Bacchaus would have to give a minimum of three months notice before flaying off his skin to use for upholstering any thread bare furniture.

'Sire, the er prisoner,' Bugflug wasn't sure if prisoner was the correct terminology. 'The er, prisoner has been transferred over to your own personal dungeon as requested.'

Bacchaus slowly raised his head from the documents he was studying at his desk. The furthest edge of his lip rose a fraction, in the Demon's version of a beaming smile.

'Good.'

'Oh and you have received a parcel from Iscyrus, my lord.'

Bacchaus indicated Bugflug to bring it forward with a hand gesture.

'It er, appears to be ice-cream, sire.'

'Yes it is symbolic.'

'Symbolic sire?'

'Yes it is symbolic. What is sweet and a dish best served cold?'

'Er, ice-cream sire.'

'Yes ice-cream and?'

'I don't understand sire.'

Bacchaus gave a long drawn out sigh. 'Revenge.'

'Oh.'

'Iscyrus has been on a little vengeance errand for me. This ice-cream is to inform me that I've had my revenge.'

'Well that's good isn't it sire. It's mint choc chip too.'

Not long to go before my probation is over now thought Bugflug.

'You may go,' said Bacchaus opening the container.

Bugflug glanced at his watch as he turned to leave. Only ten minutes left and his probation period was over. His optimistic nature told him he was going to do it. Optimists are rare in Hell and for a good reason.

'Bugflug, wait a minute,' commanded Bacchaus.

'Yes sire?'

'This ice-cream appears to have melted. It is more like a milkshake than ice-cream.'

'Ah yes sorry sire, ice-cream does tend to melt here in Hell I'm afraid. What with it being so hot. There was nothing I could do, my lord.'

'Yes of course. Most unfortunate that. You coming to the end of your probation and all.'

'Sire?'

'Oh no matter,' replied Bacchaus casually waving his hand in the air. 'I require a new rug for the fireplace anyway.'

'Well I hear Haberson's have a rug sale on at the moment.'

Bacchaus looked closely at Bugflug and shook his head. Ah, optimists he thought, they never learn.

*****

Archangel Michael sat at his desk and pulled a large, black, leather-bound book towards him. It was the sort of book that the word tome suited. With an expertise the Archangel flicked briskly though the pages to the section he was looking for. He laid a ruler down across the page and slowly, deliberately, drew a neat black line with his quill pen through one of the names listed. Adjacent to the name he wrote the word reborn in his flowing script. Taking a sheet of blotting paper he dapped up the excess ink and closed the book with a mournful sigh.

A knock at the door broke his moments reflection.

'Enter.'

A tall skinny, black haired Angel entered.

'Just thought you'd like to know sir, the plague has been retrieved and placed in a secure location.'

No doubt in a clearly marked jar labelled do not touch and placed on a top shelf out of the reach of wandering hands, thought the Archangel.

'Very good,' responded Michael his eyes remaining firmly fixed upon the book. 'If you could arrange for Death 221 to come and see me in the week. I'd like a full report. In the meantime if you could send out a list of commendations for all those involved on a job well done.'

'At once sir. Oh one other thing. It's about the Angel.'

'Jenny.'

'Sorry sir?'

'The Angel's name was Jenny.'

'Oh yes right. Well they never recovered the Angel Jenny's body.

'Why not?' A slight touch of anger broke into the Archangel's voice.

'Well, er, it wasn't there.'

'Not there?'

'Yes sir, not there. No sign of her sir.'

Archangel Michael looked up sharply. Then with a rapid blur of movement pressed the intercom button.

'Mr Moneypenny, I want you to cancel all of this afternoon's appointments. And I need to speak with The Oracle. Immediately!'

Coming Soon...

Escape From Hades

First they saved the Earth from an apocalyptic invasion. Then they saved mankind from a deadly plague. Now Death 221 and his team face their biggest challenge to date; to rescue an innocent from the very depths of Hell. You'd think they'd have found someone better for the job by now, wouldn't you?

www.ingramcontent.com/pod-product-compliance
Lightning Source LLC
LaVergne TN
LVHW051044080426
835508LV00019B/1686
9780992980313